Black Earth City

Black Earth City

A Year in the Heart of Russia

CHARLOTTE HOBSON

Granta Books
London

Granta Publications, 2/3 Hanover Yard, London N1 8BE

First published in Great Britain by Granta Books 2001

The author and publisher would like to thank the following:
Nadezhda Mandelstam: Extract from *Hope Against Hope*, first published in Great
Britain by the Harvill Press in 1971 © Nadezhda Mandelstam. English translation
© Atheneum, New York and the Harvill Press, London 1970. Reproduced by kind
permission of The Harvill Press. Osip Mandelstam, *The Voronezh Notebooks Poems
1935–1937*, translated by Richard and Elizabeth McKane, Bloodaxe Books, 1996.
Penguin UK for permission to extract two lines from *The Master and Margarita* by
Mikhail Bulgakov, translated by Richard Peaver and Larissa Volokhonsky
(Penguin Classics, 1997) copyright © by Richard Peaver and Larissa
Volokhonsky, 1997. Alan Sillitoe, 'Love in the Environs of Voronezh', *Collected
Poems*, HarperCollins Publishers Ltd, 1993. Aleksandr Blok, 'The Scythians', *The
Twelve and Other Poems*, edited by John Stallworthy and Peter France, Random
House New York, 1970. D.M. Thomas, for two lines from his translation of
'Requiem' by Anna Akhmatova; Stanley Kunitz and Max Hayward, for 'Voronezh'
by Anna Akhmatova from *Poems of Akhmatova*, Collins and Harvill Press, London,
1974. Madame Jarintsov, for the extract from *The Russians and their Language*, 1919.
G.M. Hyde, for lines from his translation of 'A Cloud in Trousers' by Vladimir
Mayakovsky in *How are Verses Made*, The Bristol Press, 1990.

A CIP catalogue record for this book is available from the British Library.

1 3 5 7 9 10 8 6 4 2

ISBN 1 86207 399 6

Typeset by M Rules

Printed and bound in Great Britain by Mackays of Chatham PLC

Many people were kind to me while I was writing this book. I am grateful to all those whose spare rooms and kitchen tables provided me with an office: to my father, to Jonathan and Heather, to Emma and Giles, and to Alexander Hoare, whose view ensured that my progress was slow but enjoyable. Selina encouraged me to begin. Will, Emily, Roly, Claire and Vitali took the trouble to comb through the manuscript in the final stages. Georgia Garrett's good judgement and good company, along with Neil Belton's enthusiasm and meticulous editing, made writing the book a pleasure. And above all, Philip's staunch support, his tact, wit and literary intuition have helped me more than I can say.

As for my friends from Voronezh, both Russian and English, it is because of them that this book exists at all. Discretion has led me to change most of the names and some of the details; otherwise I have done my best to capture our life together accurately. If there are mistakes, I hope they will forgive me. Thanks to all of you, and in particular to M.P., to whom this book is dedicated with affection.

Contents

1   Arrival   1

2   Hostel No. 4   14

3   Memorial Wood   27

4   Bourgeois Medicine   38

5   The Triangle Player   57

6   Russian Lessons   73

7   The Truth Game   84

8   Dmitri Donskoy and the Borders of Russia   99

9   Free Day   105

10 New Year, New Happiness   116

11 The House of the Deaf and Dumb   132

12 Little Pavlik   144

13 Inflation Fever   150

14 The Commission Shop   166
15 International Women's Day   179
16 The Thaw   194
17 Iron Boots   206
18 Peter Truth   221
19 Leaving   233
    Glossary   241

· 1 ·

Arrival

BBC Breakfast News
19 August 1991: 6 a.m.

On the screen, tanks rolled silently through a leafy boulevard in north Moscow.

'Mikhail Gorbachev is no longer in charge of the Soviet Union,' the newsreader was saying. It was the early-morning rush hour and yellow buses were weaving in and out, dodging the gun barrels. Commuters pressed their faces against the windows and gaped. 'Within the past three hours, the Soviet news agency Tass has announced that Mr Gorbachev cannot continue in office because of the state of his health. All power has been transferred to a right-wing Emergency Committee, headed by Vice-President Gennady Yanaev. Tanks have been moving towards the centre of Moscow for several hours.

Russian television and radio stations are broadcasting only the Emergency Committee's announcement and' – the camera cut, suddenly, to show the *corps de ballet* in *Swan Lake* pattering across a stage in their tutus – 'Tchaikovsky and Chopin. This appears to be a military coup.'

There was a time before I went to school when my mother and I visited Russia once a week. 'Welcome to Russia,' the lady always said. It was an overheated flat just outside Southampton, full of photographs of ballet dancers. In Russia's front room, where I was sent to play, two unfriendly, stiff-legged pugs lay snoring on the carpet. I didn't object, however, because of the miraculous house that sat on top of the television. It had gingerbread walls and spun sugar icicles hanging off the roof and its path was paved with chocolates and lined with jelly flowers. While my mother declined Russian nouns, I climbed up on a chair and passed the time in awed and loving contemplation of the house. She always bribed me not to touch it. 'A Curly Wurly on the way home if you leave the house alone.' Every week the temptation was too great. A little piece of the back wall and an icicle or two would disappear, and she and the lady emerged at the end of her lesson to find sugary smears across my cheeks and a welling of guilty tears. Thus I discovered that Russia was forbidden, and that it tasted of gingerbread.

My mother never gave up her Russian lessons. Between driving four children to school, delivering stews to her parents, knitting jerseys like hairy beasts and cooking for a stream of guests, she would pull a tattered exercise book out of her handbag and memorise Russian vocabulary. Sometimes she taught me a few words: *snyeg idyot* – 'it's snowing' – sounded like little hooves. On Saturday mornings, I'd climb into her bed while she did her homework. Lying in the curve of her waist and watching the strange letters flow from her green felt-tip, I pondered the information that my grandfather Igor was born in a yellow house in Moscow and bound in swaddling clothes. We had an icon from that house, a Madonna encased in silver-gilt with glass jewels in her crown, and Russian Easter eggs made of wax with velvet ribbons. All of these and my grandfather, wrapped like a swiss roll: I turned the images over in my head and grinned to myself under the bedclothes.

My mother was born Tatyana Vinogradoff, a little girl with white-blonde hair and a blue-eyed, smooth-cheeked look that later made my heart leap a hundred times when I recognised it on the street in Russia. She came from a Muscovite family of academics and teachers; her grandfather, Pavel Gavrilovich Vinogradoff, taught at Moscow University until he moved to Britain and became Professor of Jurisprudence at Oxford in 1903. In the black-and-white photograph on my mother's desk he had a statuesque quality that made it hard to believe he'd ever really lived.

If Russia meant anyone real to me, it meant my mother's father, Grandpa Igor, a large, square, adorable man with a walking stick that he wielded for emphasis. In his youth he had a passionate temperament, and once my father met a man who remembered him at university: 'Ah, dear Igor . . . the only fellow who'd come for a drink and eat the glass.'

In the nineteen twenties, he'd fought a duel with sabres; a couple of decades later, so the story went, he wrestled Lucian Freud to the ground and bit him on the ankle. By the time I knew him, he was an affectionate, learned old man with a habit of repeating his remarks three times over. 'Dear girl,' he called me, 'dear girl. Dear girl.' On one occasion, he was surprised to find that the shops were shut.

'It's Good Friday, Igor,' he was told.

'Oh,' said Igor. 'Poor chap. Poor chap. Poor chap.'

It was Igor who first suggested a dark side to Russia. When I was seven he told me – perhaps, in his absent-minded way, forgetting whom he was talking to – that children in the Soviet Union were taught to inform on their parents at school. By the time they came home their mothers and fathers were gone, vanished into the camps.

'But why?' I demanded.

'Because that's how the Bolsheviks operate,' Igor answered, thumping his stick on the floor.

Igor had good reason to hate the Communist Party. All the relations that the Vinogradoffs left behind when they moved to Oxford were dead by 1931. Four of Igor's five uncles and four of his cousins died in the civil war. His only surviving aunt, Lisa, the headmistress of a girls' school in Moscow, starved to death by the end of the twenties. Her letters simply stopped arriving.

The Vinogradoffs were typical Moscow *intelligenty*,

professors and teachers, supporters of constitutional reform. They belonged to the moderate, professional middle class that was just beginning to assert itself in Russia at the end of the nineteenth century – a class that the Bolsheviks destroyed with great thoroughness. The figure that surfaced most often in my dreams was poor Lisa, who starved. I imagined her becoming weak and her stomach swelling up. I think it struck me particularly that such a fate should befall a headmistress.

My mother's hopes that I would learn Russian at school came to nothing. The Russian teacher left because of lack of demand and I lost interest when I became a teenager. I avoided the thought of Russia; in fact I avoided thought of any kind. My mother was ill, my life was flying past in a daze. After my grandfather Igor waved his stick at Miss Hunter and insisted that our history books were full of Bolshevik propaganda, Russia lodged itself firmly in the category of things that made my toes curl. When the time came to apply for university, Arabic occurred to me as a safe choice. I had no family connections with the Arab world; surely none of them would be able to embarrass me there.

And then my mother died. She'd had cancer. It was not sudden, and yet I was a seventeen-year-old in a daydream, who'd assumed such a thing was not possible.

Eighteen months later I arrived in Edinburgh and found my way to the Department of Arabic, a little Georgian terrace on Buccleuch Place. The professor was welcoming. 'Come in, come in,' he bustled. 'Arabic honours, isn't that right?'

'That's what I want to talk to you about,' I stammered. 'I'm afraid I've changed my mind. I don't want to read Arabic after all.'

'Oh lord,' said the professor. 'Bang goes the funding for our language assistant.'

So at last I did as my mother wanted, and began to learn Russian.

19 August 1991: 8 a.m.

'... Developments in Moscow have been reverberating on the financial markets around the world. In Tokyo stocks plunged at the announcement of Mr Gorbachev's removal from power. In Hong Kong the Hang Seng index has also fallen sharply. The dollar is up, as usual benefiting from uncertain times, and gold, that traditional safe haven, has also risen. And now, Martin Sixsmith in Moscow ...'

'We have now heard that Gorbachev is in fact under arrest at his dacha in the Crimea.' The BBC's Moscow correspondent was looking pale. 'The Russian Parliament have declared that the announcement of a State of Emergency is not constitutional. Boris Yeltsin, in the Russian parliament building, seems to be gathering resistance around him. He is proposing a national strike. ... There is a substantial lobby that wants to return to the rule of Communism, and also a lobby that considers Gorbachev wasn't going fast enough. The Soviet people will be split along these lines. I think clashes will be inevitable.'

'I'm bound to say, it seems to me this will lead to violence and bloodshed,' said a commentator back in the studio. 'The coup leaders include the Prime Minister, the Minister of Defence and the head of the KGB, so one has to say that they control the forces of coercion. . . . On the other hand there will be some very serious resistance.'

My friend Emily rang halfway through the morning, having talked to our tutors at Edinburgh. 'We can forget leaving for Russia in a fortnight,' she reported. 'They think it looks bad.'

I still had not moved from in front of the television. I'd covered many eventualities in my preparations for this journey, but a military coup was not one of them.

In early 1991, I had received a letter offering me a place on a year-long course at Voronezh University, which would count towards my degree at Edinburgh. Enclosed with the letter was a list of the other students who had been accepted and a briefing document, giving detailed advice as to how to survive in the provincial town where I had decided to spend the coming months.

Voronezh was not, perhaps, the most obvious choice. When Emily and I began to look into studying in Russia, we discovered that only two universities were willing to take us for a whole year: Moscow or Voronezh, and there was a certain consensus of opinion as to which of the pair would be preferable.

'Voronezh?' said the Russians I asked, incredulously. 'Have

you any *idea* what knuckle-headed louts live in the provinces? You are a cultured person, of course you must go to Moscow.'

I talked to people with business interests in Russia. 'Well, Voronezh is somewhat – how to put it – off the map,' they hedged. 'If you go to Moscow, you're likely to end up with some useful contacts. There's a great ex-pat community there now. There's even an Irish bar.'

Emily and I were not convinced. We weren't going to Russia to sit in Irish bars and make contacts. Our minds were finally made up, however, by a girl we met from the Russian department at St Andrews. Tossing back her hair, she began to talk about the coming year.

'I'm going to Moscow, actually,' she said. 'Are you coming too? Oh, it's going to be such fun. A whole bunch of my friends are coming, we've got the maddest ideas. We're organising a ball! You absolutely must come. We'll all be living in the same hostel, so I'll know where to find you.'

Emily and I did not need to confer. 'Actually, we're going to Voronezh,' we said politely, in unison. Isn't this how all the most important decisions are made?

Russian Language Universities Scheme briefing document issued for Voronezh:

An average-sized city (pop: 1 million) situated on the banks of the river Voronezh, 8 km north of its confluence with the mighty river Don. It lies some 500 km SSE of Moscow, or approximately halfway between Moscow and the Black Sea, on the border between the forest and meadow region of middle Russia, and the southern steppe. The soil is famously fertile, owing to the prevalence of black earth. The potato is the major crop of the region and among the finest in all Russia.

Founded in 1586 as a Cossack fort against Tartar raids, Voronezh soon became an important entrepôt for corn and other produce carried up the Don from the southern regions. Since Soviet times, it has flourished as an industrial centre producing a wide range of products, including televisions, chocolates and nuclear power. The city contains a monument to Peter the Great, a railway college, two museums and a well-regarded university. Almost completely destroyed during the Great Patriotic War of 1940–45, during which it suffered front-line fighting for two hundred days, the city has been rebuilt in the finest tradition of Soviet construction and design . . .

After several paragraphs in this vein, the tone became practical. 'Certain items will be invaluable to you in Voronezh. The correct clothing is essential, as in winter the temperature falls to minus twenty and more.' A sports shop sold me a pair of fur-lined boots a size too large and a down-filled coat that, they said, was suitable even for a hanging bivouac. (They showed me a photograph: a climber dangling from a snowy peak in a kind of sling made of Goretex.) 'In summer the temperature can be as high as forty degrees. In the autumn it is rainy and muddy.' Three cases were already full. 'Necessities will be hard to find in Voronezh.' So Emily and I stocked up. We bought two saucepans and a frying pan, plates, mugs, cutlery, coffee, teabags, tomato paste, dried milk, dried mushrooms, packet soup, a Christmas pudding, vitamins, stock cubes, marmite and ten packets of Sainsbury's luxury nut selection. We bought a year's supply of toothpaste, soap, tampax, shampoo, toilet paper, aspirin, plasters, antibiotics and a sterile surgical pack with a full set of syringes and a drip. We bought presents, without knowing who they were to be for: tins of Earl Grey tea, Union Jack ashtrays, postcards of Princess Diana and a joke nose on elastic. When we'd got these home, we went straight out again and bought bleach, a padlock, cockroach powder, contraceptives, a rape alarm, a scrubbing brush, a pair of flip-flops each and an Allen key which was necessary, apparently, to open the windows on Russian trains. I never actually remembered to take it with me on a train journey but it had a talismanic value. Surely I was ready for every possible situation now that I had an Allen key.

Prepare yourself, above all, for a year in a remote and underdeveloped city. The post takes six weeks to arrive. To make an international telephone call, you must queue at the central Telegraph Office for several hours. There is little entertainment other than that which you make yourselves.

A stereo, a backgammon set and a sandwich toaster joined the pile. To qualify, books had to be more than five hundred pages long: *The Brothers Karamazov*, *The Anatomy of Melancholy*, *The Master and Margarita*, *The Seven Pillars of Wisdom* and several weighty biographies filled another case. At the last moment, Emily decided she couldn't bear to suffer from her bad back for a year, and packed up a double futon, five foot square, made by the blind in Dundee. We each had a baggage allowance of twenty-two kilos; between us, what with the futon, our luggage must have weighed more than a hundred. And then the tanks rolled into Moscow.

19 August 1991: 11 a.m.

A breezy, efficient woman called Felicity Cave was in charge of the scheme with Russian universities; from my seat in front of the television I tried her telephone number throughout the day. It was engaged. In Moscow the weather was still and humid. The Special Forces soldiers surrounding the television centre had faces tense and shiny with sweat.

At about four o'clock, tanks arrived outside the Russian parliament building, known as the White House, where Boris Yeltsin and his supporters had established themselves. For a quarter of an hour the tanks pointed their guns at the White House, engines running. Inside, the only real opposition to the coup was at the Emergency Committee's mercy. There was only a small number of people watching, and yet the tanks hesitated.

Suddenly Yeltsin walked out of the White House. Alone, without bodyguards, he approached one of the tanks and clambered on top of it. He shook hands with the soldiers inside and turned to his spectators.

'Citizens of Russia,' he shouted. 'The legally elected president of the country has been removed from power. . . . We are dealing with a right-wing, reactionary, anti-constitutional coup d'état . . .' The crowd cheered.

Soon afterwards Felicity Cave answered the telephone. I should have known it would take more than a coup to flummox her. Her cheerful tones trumpeted down the line like the hunting horn across the valleys.

'Tanks? Never mind the tanks! Of course you'll be going, just as planned! All be over in two or three days, take my word for it.'

And she was right. For two days we watched as demonstrators collected around the White House. On Monday night, a crowd of thousands spent the night outside, behind the rickety barricades. The tone on the BBC was still sombre. We had seen the coup leaders looking shaky and indecisive at a press conference, but seven months earlier, in Vilnius, we had also seen Russian tanks firing on the crowds surrounding the television tower.

Fifty thousand people were outside the White House on Tuesday night, when the tanks were expected to move against the parliament. Then, just as the liberals looked in the greatest danger, the coup collapsed. The troops were ordered back to barracks and the plotters were arrested, except for the

Interior Minister, Pugo, who killed himself. An aged, shaken Gorbachev returned from the Crimea, and Yeltsin was acclaimed as the saviour of Russia.

At the end of the month, Emily and I met in London and celebrated. The Soviet Union had fallen to pieces. Ukraine had declared its independence from Moscow on 24 August, and Belorussia had followed a day later, changing its name to Belarns. Moldova left on 26 August, Azerbaijan on the 30th. The Communist Party, which had governed these vast lands since 1917, had been dissolved. Officials who had collaborated with the coup were under arrest, Party property was seized and *Pravda*, the Party organ, was closed down. Gorbachev was unemployed. Yeltsin was trying to reform the system and there was a mood of wild optimism on the streets.

None of this momentous news, however, was the main cause for joy. Emily and I drank red wine at her house and played a song by the Waterboys called 'Red Army Blues'. 'Took a train to Voronezh,' it went, 'it was as far as we could go.' We had our visas. In a week we would already have arrived.

· 2 ·

Hostel No. 4

They're light-minded . . . well, what of it . . . mercy
sometimes knocks at their hearts . . . ordinary people . . .
only the housing problem has corrupted them.

Mikhail Bulgakov, *The Master and Margarita*

Hostel No. 4 teemed with activity, most of it verminous.
Cockroaches swarmed through the building unchecked; they
inhabited the central heating system and the warm, juddering
fridge motors in every room. In the kitchens were piles of
rubbish two foot high that rustled in the dark. The light bulbs
in the toilets were always being stolen, making the fauna in
there difficult to identify; but the occasional shouts of horror
from people picking their way through the darkness were tes-
timony to its existence.

The human overpopulation was equally intense. There
were at least three and often closer to six people to each room,
in which the occupants slept, worked, had parties, ate, drank,
sulked, wrote letters, cooked, smoked and hung out their
washing. In Room 179, which Emily and I shared with Ira, a
kind, velvety-eyed girl from a town in the Voronezh region,

our belongings were thrust under the beds and into two thin, coffin-shaped cupboards by the door. The fridge chugged like an idling truck. The Voronezh-made television, which Ira turned on as soon as she woke up, crackled and buzzed. The brand-new orange wallpaper peeled gently away from the walls, and the rug we bought from the Univermag gave off puffs of red and purple powder at every tread.

Less than a week had passed since I'd stepped off the train with our group of thirty British students into the pale sunshine of a Voronezh morning. The clock had struck nine as we looked around us at the yellow station dozing in the dust.

'On time exactly,' the *Komendant*, head of the hostel, had smiled, as our luggage was loaded onto a cart. 'Our railway system has not yet adjusted to our new political situation.'

We followed him over the tram tracks, up the street, and into a yard in which stray dogs were picking over a pile of smouldering rubbish. In front of us stood a squat, flat-fronted block: Hostel No. 4. The entrance hall was underwater green; against one wall sat a babushka whose metal teeth glinted in the half-light. Heaps of rubble lay in the corners. On the fourth floor, halfway down the corridor, Emily and I were shown into a long, low room, empty but for three iron bed-frames. The stink of the rust-coloured paint that had been splashed over the ceiling and the grimy lino floor rose up to meet us, along with a stale, sweaty smell. There was a pause.

'I'm sure we can improve it,' I ventured.

Emily did not reply. At last I glanced at her. She was laughing: her silent, hysterical laugh that possessed her so completely, there was no breath left even to wheeze. I could see what she meant.

A few days later, however, term began and the place was transformed. Ira arrived and our room filled up. Out in the bottle-green corridor, a crowd appeared, chatting, cooking, scrounging cigarettes, offering KGB telephones or medals or icons for sale. At any time, half of them were drunk and the other half had a hangover. Occasionally there were scuffles; sometimes the *Komendant* walked past in a lordly way and was bombarded with requests. It was a cosmopolitan place, housing more than twenty nationalities. The majority still were Russian, yet on our floor alone were Syrians, Egyptians and Armenians as well as British, and one Italian, sent half-crazy by Russian food. Downstairs were Angolans, Nigerians, East Germans; New Yorkers visited from other hostels, and Venezuelans studying forestry, Georgians, Uzbeks and Cossacks. A hubble of languages rose through the smoke and pungent smells of ten dinners cooking in one kitchen; twenty stereos roared out different tastes in music. If it were not for the determined ugliness of the place, we might have been in an Anatolian bazaar. There was no doubt that it had a certain filthy charm.

The hostel residents had simple priorities. Food, for one. It was scarce that year; the shops had an echoing, dusty feel, and even the tins of corned beef labelled 'EC: Humanitarian Aid' were marked up in price each week, according to infla-tion. The Italian boy saw it as a challenge, and day after day set off to scour the city, returning triumphant and exhausted with a piece of lean beef or some ripe tomatoes. With the regular supplies of tinned Italian butter, olive oil, arborio rice and so on that his family sent him from Milan, he managed to get by. The rest of us more or less gave up eating and concentrated instead on the second priority: drink. Vodka was so much simpler to get hold of, and there was juice to drink with it for the health-conscious. The third priority was really the most pressing. Beyond eating and drinking, entertainment was needed, mental and physical exercise and inspiration. Sex, above all, preoccupied Hostel No. 4. Soon I began to notice the couples circling the hostel in search of an empty room.

'Are you going out?' they'd hiss. 'Lend us your room, just for half an hour.'

But even half an hour of privacy was not easily available. Some resorted to kissing on the stairs and in the corridors, oblivious of the bustle; or their roommates would return from ten minutes in the shower to find the door locked, and no amount of knocking and pleading would persuade those inside to open up. Those couples who were stricken by modesty had nowhere. Hotels were impossible – apart from the expense, you needed some kind of official chit to book a room – and outside, despite the blue skies, the wind was cold and insistent. Thus a heady strain of unrequited desire added spice to our communal claustrophobia.

One sunny afternoon, a man built in the Socialist Realist mould knocked at our door. His gaunt, wedge-shaped head and chips of blue glass for eyes gave him an air of steely dedication, while the six-foot-four frame filling our doorway suggested a character who would stop at nothing. He produced a bottle of vodka and said in a voice from the grave, 'Let's get acquainted.'

Viktor, he told us, was his name. Emily and I introduced ourselves, and we all drank a large shot of vodka. We began to talk, using a mixture of broken Russian and English. But somehow after every few minutes, Viktor would apologise and interrupt.

'I'm sorry,' he said. 'I've forgotten what you are called . . . ah, yes! Now let's drink to our acquaintance.'

In our innocence we kept on telling him our names, earnestly spelling them out, until we were halfway through the bottle. Viktor looked as though he might be suppressing a smirk. 'Your names? I just can't seem to keep them in my head.'

It was a challenge to keep them in my own head by then. Ira arrived back from lectures and admonished him. 'Viktor! What have you done with my *anglichanki*?'

'Baptised them,' said Viktor, grinning. 'Have a drink.'

Other people wandered in and before I'd noticed, it was a party. A couple of English boys put Ozric Tentacles on and started dancing. Ira thrust haphazard cheese toasties into the sandwich toaster. Viktor made a trip to the railway station for more vodka and returned with three girls, who burst into the room talking and gesticulating with cigarettes and, in one hand, a kitten.

'These are the girls from Room 99,' Viktor explained. 'Nina, Tanya, and the tall girl is known as Liza Minelli – well, you can see why.'

'Who's a brave little bunny?' said Liza Minelli to the kitten. She had the hair and spider-leg eyelashes of her heroine. 'Tanya, over there, she's its mother. It'll be lucky if it survives, poor little thing.'

She glowered at Tanya, who, without stopping talking for an instant had settled down, put her feet on the table, and opened a new bottle. Nina was giggling and squeaking on each inhalation.

'Pay no attention,' Viktor murmured. 'Liza Minelli is furious with the other two; you see, she and Nina have fallen for the same man.'

'So why is she angry with Tanya?' I asked.

Viktor shrugged. 'Just because.'

'Ladies, gentlemen, small cats,' Tanya announced. 'A toast – to this university year. May it bring all of us exactly what we want.'

Her roommates looked daggers at each other, and Viktor laughed. '*Otdykh*,' he said. It was his favourite word, meaning relaxation in its widest sense, with associations of the long, peaceful exhalation one makes after downing a glass of vodka. On Viktor's lips it spoke of pleasure in all its forms: a long-awaited cigarette, a summer breeze, the seduction of some unsuspecting girl. As I came to know Viktor better, I realised that my first impression of a man with a cause was not so mistaken. His life was a quest for *otdykh*, and his dedication did much to persuade the rest of the hostel down the same path.

After a while, a slight, attractive boy with floppy hair pushed his head around the door. 'Hi everyone,' he muttered.

'Yakov!' cried Liza Minelli, holding out her hands to him. 'Come in.'

'Hi Yakov,' said Nina, patting the chair beside her. 'Sit here with me.'

He was obviously the lucky guy. He smiled a little goofily, pleased with himself, and sat between them. It didn't look as though he had much option.

Another crowd of people arrived, including some Americans from a different hostel, and we drank several more toasts. Someone turned the lights off. The party was really hotting up now; I could see at least three couples in sweaty embrace and Tanya seemed to be taking her clothes off in the corner. 'Is that your roommate over there?' said someone in my ear. It was a muscly, dark-eyed Russian in flip-flops, pointing at Emily. 'Viktor and me, we think she's incredibly attractive.'

'Oh, yes, she's great, she –'

He'd already gone, squeezing across the room towards her. I found myself talking to a large American boy with red curly hair and freckles. 'It's always been hard for me to fit in,' he was saying. 'I guess it's because I'm black.'

'You're black?'

'Albino. I have black features, you see, but Scottish colouring. My name's Sasha McDuff.'

Out of the corner of my eye I could see Emily chatting to

Viktor and her other admirer. Ira was giggling with one of the English boys, Joe, who was trying to feed her pieces of toasted cheese sandwich. Someone fell over, bringing down the washing line.

'I call myself Sasha now because I feel that Russia's my spiritual home,' the American was telling me. 'It's very important for me to feel that I'm making progress towards a more solid sense of identity.'

'I see –'

Suddenly Liza Minelli turned the lights on. All the couples on the beds sat up, blinking, and Tanya hastily put her knickers back on. 'That's enough,' said Liza Minelli. 'Everyone, you'll have to listen to me for a moment. I've borne this for too long. He –' she pointed one trembling finger at Yakov – 'will have to make his choice.'

'Me?' Yakov looked startled.

'Oh for God's sake, can't you just sort this out among yourselves?'

'No!' barked Liza Minelli. 'I want witnesses. Then he can't go back on his word.'

'All right then,' said Tanya. 'Yakov, who's it to be?'

'*Bozhe moi*,' Yakov gulped. 'I don't know if I can . . .'

'Why not?' Nina said indignantly. 'What about the things you said to me last night?'

There was a quiver of anticipation from the audience.

'Choose, you bastard,' said a few female voices.

'Don't say a thing! Don't let the women bully you into it!' said the blokes.

'Is anyone willing to take a bet?' hissed Joe. 'I'll put a thousand roubles on the blonde.'

'Yakov, look at me,' said Liza Minelli. She spread her hands out before her, palms upwards. 'Everything that I have, I give to you. My heart, my soul . . .'

The audience went crazy. Yakov hesitated, and turned. 'Nina?' he enquired.

Nina giggled in that way that she did, squeaking with each inhalation. 'Come on, *milenky*,' she said, taking his arm. 'Let's go. Sorry, Liza.'

They left and Liza Minelli turned on her heel and rushed down the corridor in the other direction. Someone turned the lights back off and the party resumed. After that, Yakov and Nina were another couple to be found sloping around the hostel looking for an empty room. Liza Minelli got over the whole affair quite quickly. She had a kind disposition beneath the melodrama. The only time she got annoyed was when she got back from lectures to find the door of Room 99 locked; then she'd come upstairs to visit us and curse the pair of them.

The hostel had a well-deserved reputation for low morals. In its defence, however, it must be said that a sexual revolution was taking place all over Russia. The Communist regime was prudish in the extreme. Of course men had affairs, that was normal, but women were expected to behave nicely – not smoke in public, for example, or wear short skirts. As for any hint of open licentiousness, despite what went on behind the scenes in Party dachas – it was considered antisocial and dealt with severely.

Now, suddenly, the controls disappeared and seventy years of pent-up desire burst onto the streets. Voronezh at that time was far more liberal than London. Pornographic magazines and crotchless knickers were for sale at every bus stop. The morning news programme might show a woman giving birth, and soft porn dominated the airwaves in the evening. Even the babushkas exchanged their string shopping bags for new, Polish-made plastic with naked lovelies on each side.

The Proletariat cinema on Revolution Prospect, meanwhile, revelling in its new freedom, dug out all the films it had not been allowed to show and billed them as 'classics' and 'great entertainment for all'. The selection was unpredictable. *Night Porter*, in a fuzzy seventies print that made Dirk Bogarde's face look orange, caused its final sensation here in Voronezh where it was advertised on a huge hand-painted board as 'New! Shocking! Erotica!' One week there would be a season of Fellini or Bunuel; the next you might find yourself watching *Caligula*, probably the only movie that Sir John Gielgud made in association with Penthouse Films. I was left with the distinct feeling that Sir John had not been shown this version of the film, in which chunks of soft porn had been spliced alongside the cinematic Ancient Rome that is familiar to us all. Billed as 'educational' and screened by the Proletariat at seven o'clock on a weekday, it played to the usual crowd of middle-aged couples on an evening out. Half an hour into the film, there were so many people walking out that you couldn't see the screen. Not everybody approved of the new climate.

In the Voronezh papers there was an air of bewilderment. Where had all this filth sprung from? How was it that a poll of teenage girls, who five years previously had held only one ambition – to be Lenin's little helper – now answered overwhelmingly that when they were grown up, they wanted to be a hard-currency prostitute? For the time being, however, even the most choleric voices tailed away into resignation. It was inevitable, after all, that Western decadence would arrive along with glasnost, said the pessimistic characters in the butter queue. They're only young, rejoined others comfortably. Let them enjoy themselves while they can. Lord knows we did just the same, although it was all a secret back then.

As winter approached and the rising prices began to pinch, in the hostel a few girls made a policy decision. Lena was an energetic girl who cleaned her room every afternoon in a baggy purple tracksuit. In the evenings, she left the hostel in a wig, miniskirt, fishnets and stilettos for the Brno Hotel, where she entertained businessmen from the Baltics and Tashkent. She was the kindest, smiliest girl, always willing to oblige. She'd lend you a saucepan if your own had gone missing, and one afternoon in Room 99 when Emily and the girls were almost expiring of boredom and poverty, Lena stripped to cheer them up. She must have given a great deal of pleasure to those businessmen. The only person who was not always happy was her English roommate. 'I just don't understand it,' she used to complain. 'She's got a terrible lot of menfriends.'

It was hard to support oneself on a student grant, and most people relied on their parents for food. Lola, whose parents lived in the Crimea, depended instead on what she referred to as aid from Africa. She had a Somalian boyfriend in the next-door hostel who used to cook her a lovely hot meal after they'd had sex. The point was that it was usually a meaty dish, while the rest of the hostel was living on candy-pink sausage meat, rumoured to be rat. 'We had beef,' she'd say, smiling complacently when she returned. She was a compact little person, but she liked her dinner.

In Room 99, poor Tanya had broken her leg, which prompted the girls to begin a blockade diary on the wall:

Oct. 5   Spent last money on vodka for anaesthetic for Tanya.

Oct. 15   Collected student grant – 92 roubles – enough for 18 packets of cigarettes. How will we survive the month?

Oct. 20   Only half a sausage left. Don't know if we can afford to keep on feeding the invalid . . .

In fact the atmosphere was cheerful, for despite the prospect of starvation, the hostel air was having its effect. Yakov and Nina were together; Ira, up in our room, had instantly fallen for Joe, the boy she ate cheese toasties with at that first party, and for the rest of the year they sank into a happy, soporific passion fuelled by cannabis. Tanya was stepping out with an English boy, as far as the leg in plaster permitted. And Emily, my main ally, had finally been won over by Yuri, a sophisticated, funny boy who had swept aside her other admirers.

I found myself alone in Room 179 one evening. It was close to midnight and I could no longer concentrate on my book. The bulb overhead gave off a greyish, shadowless light, barely illuminating the piles of clutter, the washing on the line, the layer of dust. The fridge shuddered violently and fell silent, as though for ever. It was very quiet. Only a little creaking noise could be heard occasionally as the wallpaper peeled away from the walls. I listened hard. Surely I was not the only person who heard this tiny, insistent beat, the pulse of hostel couplings. *Creak-creak. Creak-creak.* It began slowly, then picked up speed. *Creak-creak. Creak-creak.* The walls were pulsing too; the whole building was joyfully, mindlessly joining in the rhythm.

I pulled the blanket over my head and tried to go to sleep.

· 3 ·

Memorial Wood

I should like to call you all by name,
But they have lost the lists.

Anna Akhmatova, 'Requiem',
written 1935–40

The forest outside Voronezh covers many miles and it is
easy to lose your way among its closely planted stands of
pine and birch. Russian families eager for mushrooms and
berries flock to it in daytime, but when the light begins to
fade and the birds fall silent they make sure to catch the
little electric train back to town. Once they are at home,
however, tasting the mushrooms fried in garlic, the conversation returns to nature and its healing properties. To our
woods – someone announces, raising a glass of vodka – how
good they are for the soul. Everyone agrees, glasses are
clinked. The massacres, after all, happened long ago; when a
secret is kept for so many years, it can almost be forgotten.

Igor Kazakov was a big, lazy, graceful man with a sense of
irony. He lay stretched out on a bed in the hostel the first time
I met him, smoking cigarette after cigarette, saying little. It

was late and there were empty bottles under the table by the time he mentioned the woods.

'I know a beautiful place in the forest, a camp, all on its own. A few wooden huts, and a river where we bathe after the steam bath . . .' he began slowly. 'My father and his friends built it in the sixties, when they were at university and it was all free love and the songs of Bulat Okudzhava.' Igor smiled. 'He's a cynic now, of course.'

He drew hard on a cigarette. Then he continued. 'You know how Russians are. The idea of living in the countryside is horrible, yet we have a passionate romance with nature . . . It's a nine-kilometre walk to this camp, and by the time you arrive, it's as though the city never existed. Everyone behaves differently there, they're happy . . .' He grimaced at himself and laughed. 'You should see it for yourselves.'

So on Saturday morning five of us met Igor at the station. He was carrying his guitar and a five-litre jar of marinated pork for *shashlyk*, kebabs. With him stood a boy and a dark-eyed, intense girl whom he introduced as Seryozha and Lyuba.

'When Igor rang, I said we wouldn't miss it for anything,' Lyuba told us as we headed for the train. 'We need to relax.'

'You'll see,' said Igor dryly, 'that when Lyuba relaxes, she does it properly.'

We peered out of the train windows at the city's Saturday afternoon bustle. The industrial zone on the left bank of the reservoir puffed pinkish smoke into the sky. A fishing boat chugged past the bridge, while the fisherman hurriedly prepared his bait. From the steep right-hand bank, with its jumble of wooden houses, came the busy tock-tock of home-owners engaged in renovations and on Revolution Prospect even the chess players, baking gently in the sun, looked more animated than usual. This was what Russians call the 'woman's summer', the last warm days of the year before its youth is cut short by autumn. Our little *elektrichka*, clattering along the tracks to the woods, only added to the air of hard-won holiday.

After half an hour we climbed down onto a strip of crumbling concrete and looked about us. The mid-afternoon sun made everything glow. Igor played the opening riff of one of those Russian songs that sound like a march and originate in the prisons. 'Let's go,' he called over his shoulder. 'Nine kilo-metres to the camp.'

It is hard, now, to catch the sensation of that night without later events intervening. Birches lined the road, their leaves already orange against a soaring pale blue sky. Behind them stood the dark, serried pines, growing so close as to be almost impenetrable. We occasionally passed tracks which branched off at right angles to the road; lined with identical trunks, they ran far into the distance. After three or four kilometres there was a sign by the road. The silhouette of a man's chest riddled with bullet holes stood out against a white back-ground. There was one word written underneath: MEMORIAL.

'What is it?' I asked.

'It's a sign,' said Igor.

'Igor, but what does it mean?'

'Oh, Russian politics. Lyuba knows all about it.'

Lyuba was silent for a moment. Then she said, 'It's a monument put up by the Voronezh Memorial group. My father's the president. If you're interested, I can explain it to you –'

'I'd like that –'

'But not now. I'm sorry.' She turned away. 'I hear about nothing else at home. Now let's have a drink, Seryozha, shall we? We've come to enjoy ourselves.'

The woods have many powers. Their sheer extent – stretching a quarter of the way around the world, north and east of Voronezh all the way to Vladivostok – draws you in like vertigo. One thousand million pine trees, each identical to its neighbour. How many people have vanished into their enormity? How many woodsmen live on undisturbed, unaware, perhaps, of the fall of Communism, or even of the Revolution? There were Polish partisans from the last war who did not emerge until the fifties. The Greens, Russian peasants who abandoned or were driven out of their villages in the civil war, were not quelled for a decade: they would burst out of the forest, slaughter villages or Red Army columns, and disappear.

Every Russian child knows that the woods are full of terrors. Bears, wolves, boar roam in them; mischievous and evil sprites of all kinds entice you, mislead you and drive you mad. I remember my mother telling me about the witch, Baba Yaga, who lives in the woods. By day she sleeps in a house that stands on chicken legs, surrounded by skulls with glowing eyes. By night she flies through the trees in a pestle and mortar, searching for victims. Even in the gentle English downlands, the idea was enough to keep me awake and rigid in my bed.

'Listen,' said Igor, stopping suddenly. 'Can you hear?'

In the silence I heard a thousand whispering voices.

'The woods are telling us something . . .'

'Oh, shut up, Igor!'

Igor laughed, took up his guitar again and sang.

'Akh, that evening, that evening,
When the evil wind blew . . .'

The light was fading by the time we arrived at the camp, and a huge yellow moon had risen. Seven or eight huts were clustered by a river where it widened to a form a deep pool. Mist was rising from the water in coils; behind it the ghosts of trees on the opposite bank could just be seen. We were excited and ran about, building a fire for *shashlyk* and for the steam bath. Seryozha and Lyuba had finished off the wine on the way, so that Seryozha sagged palely against a tree and fell asleep, and Lyuba was roaring drunk.

'Now who's going to pour me some vodka, lads,' she cried, swaying a little.

We spooned red caviar straight from the tin, then cooked *shashlyk* on skewers and ate them with flat Georgian bread. After we'd finished, Lyuba danced a Caucasian dance of her own invention, sat down suddenly and said, 'Hey Igor! We're going to have fun, aren't we?'

'As much as you want, Lyubochka.'

She leant across and kissed him. His arms hanging by his side, nonchalantly, he kissed her back.

'To the moon!' shouted Lyuba, raising her glass. 'To life! To oblivion!'

'To the woods . . .' said Igor, taking Lyuba's hand.

The steam bath was ready. Seryozha was shaken awake. All of us hurried, stripped naked in the damp, pine-smelling room, and entered the *banya* itself, blinded by steam. It was a little wood-lined chamber, with slatted shelves at various heights; the stove, its iron cover heated until it glowed, stood in the corner. Water was flung on and the stove let out a sharp hiss; scalded drops ran about the metal and disappeared. The room vanished. Everyone was silent, taking short breaths of the pine-smelling steam. Sweat prickled through skin. When we could bear it no longer, we plunged, shouting, through the mist to the river.

The following week I visited Lyuba and her father. At home Lyuba was neat and businesslike, whisking the books and papers she had been working on into a drawer and preparing tea. Her father, a kindly, unassuming man in a beige cardigan, beamed and asked about England, our families and so on. After a while, she interrupted.

'They've come to hear about the Memorial Wood.'

'Ah yes.' For the first time since our arrival, Lyuba's father stopped smiling. Then he went over to the desk and took various files from the drawers. 'Perhaps you have heard of our organisation?'

I had. Memorial was one of glasnost's triumphs, an organisation that emerged in Moscow in 1987 to establish information on Stalin's victims and to commemorate them. At first it was a group of perhaps fifteen human rights activists who wrote a petition demanding the right to start work on this massive task. Their acquaintances wouldn't sign, afraid that it was yet another KGB provocation. So the members of the group took to the streets to collect signatures. To their astonishment, people responded, although signing could still result in arrest. The signatures grew to hundreds, then thousands. By the end of 1988, over two hundred regional branches of Memorial had been founded, including this one in Voronezh, all dedicated to research and to putting up monuments to the dead.

'Well.' Lyuba's father wiped his kind, plump face. 'In this wood that you walked through, we have uncovered around seven hundred corpses from pits beneath the pine trees. Most of them were shot between January and March 1938 with heavy-calibre bullets to the back of the head, using Nagan revolvers, standard issue to NKVD officers. They would have been transported there from various camps in the region: Boguchar, Ostrogorsk, Sosnovka, Borisoglebsk, Novokhopirsk . . .'

'Bobrov,' added Lyuba, pouring tea.

'Bobrov too. Taken in trucks to the edge of the wood and then marched to their graves. We don't know if the NKVD prepared the graves beforehand or if the victims dug them. Here is something we found –' He passed me a battered cardboard wallet, stained and bent. It was a student identity card, the photograph inside faded almost to extinction; I could just make out a round, serious face, cropped hair. 'A boy, only nineteen . . . There were men and women of all ages, but most were less than forty years old. We have only identified a few.'

'Here,' Lyuba added, picking out another picture of a young man. 'A post office worker, accused of conducting anti-Soviet conversations with Christ. He was charged with crimes of the tongue.'

'Beniamino Ferroni.' Her father held up a photo of a dark-haired man in a suit. 'He was an Italian who ran the Voronezh circus. Shot for espionage. Please, look for yourself.'

I sifted through the papers. Among them were photographs of the objects that they had found in the graves: silver crosses, wedding rings, handcuffs. A few faded, grey-eyed faces looked out at me, expressionless, and I had a swift vision of them marching towards their graves. They must have used the same road as us.

'There were priests among them, peasants from the collective farms, apparatchiks,' said Lyuba's father. 'The KGB have prepared a list of eighteen thousand victims from the region who are now to be rehabilitated. Eighteen thousand innocent people . . . We've hardly begun our excavations. There are those who believe that the whole forest stands on the bones of Stalin's victims, not just the Memorial Wood at Dubovka. They're probably right. Where else could they have hidden thousands of dead bodies?'

There was a pause. Then he continued. 'We've fought for

this for more than two years, you know. We demanded to be allowed to see the archives. Finally they let us in. Then we demanded permission to dig. Suddenly, the KGB, the Party organs and the city council were willing to collaborate . . . an order from above. I know they still have not shown us all the records. Voronezh is a conservative place – there are those who simply think this work is unnecessary, and there are also those who think it sabotage, yet another attempt to blacken Stalin's name. But we're not going to give up.' He gazed across at the dark window, stirring more sugar into his tea. 'Well,' he sighed. 'There is to be a funeral service. You must come.'

Lyuba showed me to the door. We stood there awkwardly for a moment, until I plucked up the courage and asked her.

'What about the camp where we stayed, Lyuba. Is that ground also –'

She looked levelly at me. 'Who knows?'

Two weeks later a group of us travelled out of Voronezh to the woods again, this time by bus. The city still basked in the sun, although early autumn had already added a touch of gilded, self-conscious prettiness to the parks. It was a week-day, so most of the passengers on the bus heading for the Memorial Wood were pensioners. They carried flowers and strangely shaped bags. Some had brought their grandchildren, wrapping them up in woollies until they were scarlet in the face. Lyuba and her father were to meet us there.

We came to a halt at the edge of the woods. The sky was the

same clear, sharp blue as it had been when we arrived with Igor. Shadows danced over the tree trunks and the small crowd, and a group of children chased each other through the trees, laughing and gasping for breath. The mourners pulled home-made wreaths from their bags. Some had a photograph in the centre framed by pink and red crepe roses; others an Orthodox cross, and the letters V.P.: *vechnaya pamyat* – eternal memory. Manuscripts don't burn, as Bulgakov wrote. At first it's easy to forget. Then time creeps on, and it becomes almost impossible.

In the centre of the crowd, three priests had already begun chanting the funeral mass. Several long, high caskets lined with red cloth lay before them. The old people pushed us to the front.

'Look, look,' insisted one old man. 'You can see the bullet holes.'

They had not been able to make any attempt at separate burials; bones were jumbled together with clods of earth, twisted belt buckles, shoes, rags. Everything that had been found had gone in. The skulls were at the top, looking out, each with a neat round hole in the crown.

'Lamb of God, have mercy on us,' chanted the priests. The mourners joined in with quavering voices. Many were weep-ing, but they did not for a moment take their eyes from the bones, standing squarely in front of them and holding up their candles.

'Lamb of God, have mercy on us.'

The pines swayed a little against the sky.

'Lamb of God, grant us thy peace.'

The children playing hide and seek among the trees were breathless with giggles; a tiny boy was trying to hide behind a sapling, without realising that he was broader than it. He kept very still and squeezed his eyes shut.

4

Bourgeois Medicine

SOPHIE: Talking ill of Moscow!
   That comes of seeing the world! Where could be better?
CHATSKY: Where there are none of us.

Aleksandr Griboedov, *Woe from Wit*, 1824

A little pale sunlight was failing to compete with the blaze of autumn the day that Edik Zelyony first took me out for an ice cream. He clasped his hands behind his back and picked his way through the drifting leaves, complaining about Voronezh in his precise English. 'So small-minded. Just gossip, gossip . . . And there is no work here either. My aunt in Moscow will soon be sending for me, although of course Moscow! It's just a big village. But it's easier to go abroad from Moscow, you understand.'

When we reached the ice-cream parlour at the end of Revolution Prospect, he removed his jacket and cap, peering in the mirror at his long, thin face and bulbous eyes, straightening his spectacles. He adjusted the silk scarf around his neck minutely and ushered me to a seat, explaining, 'I'm a martyr to my throat.'

The ice cream came in steel bowls and the teaspoons had holes in, to discourage customers from taking them home. Edik put a spoonful into his coffee and drank it before it melted. 'Most of the Jews have already gone,' he said. 'The orchestras are empty all over the country . . . There are just a handful of us left.' He licked his spoon disconsolately, then cheered up. 'I'll introduce you to the Uvarovs,' he announced. 'They'll be glad to meet you. They keep an open house – you know, a salon. There you will find *le tout* Voronezh. It's their daughters, Masha and Valya – Madame Uvarova is determined to find them each a suitable husband. At the moment Valya is seeing a boy who is terribly rich – dreadfully rich. His father is building himself a house with four turrets and a jacuzzi. But you know Madame Uvarova is not satisfied, she is chasing him away little by little . . . he is not a cultured boy, you see. That is what matters to La Uvarova. Also he is fat.'

'What about you, Edik? Are you suitable?'

'Oh, I am quite a *habitué* of the household. Not enough money, you see' – he rolled his eyes – 'but cultured. The Uvarovs say, Here is Zelyony – now we shall have intelligent conversation! You will hear them say it. The provinces, you understand . . . the intelligentsia is quite suffocated here.' Gloomily, he licked the last of the ice cream from his upper lip.

That evening, back at the hostel, I sat down to write a letter. 'I've met a character straight from Chekhov!!' I scrawled, not sparing the punctuation. 'Only he's not dreaming of Moscow, but the Rîve Gauche or Bloomsbury seething with intellectuals. He's a terrible snob, vain too, but somehow a sympathetic character . . . perhaps because it feels as though I've already seen this play.'

A couple of days later there was a knock on my door and Edik walked in. 'My throat is killing me,' he greeted me piteously. 'I can barely speak. Treat me with your bourgeois medicine.'

He languished a little, while I looked through the bags under my bed. Searching through these bags took hours of my day in Voronezh. I rarely found the exact thing I was looking for, although all sorts of randomly associated, useless objects would emerge. This time I did find a packet of Lockets, but Edik dismissed them. 'Soviet-style lozenges – not real medicine.'

'Well, no, but –' I thought for a moment and took up the first thing that came to hand, which happened to be a bottle of vitamin B pills. 'You're right. You need something stronger . . . these are the thing. Take them with water. Yes, I know they don't taste good. It's because they are double strength.'

So we both set off satisfied to the Uvarovs' flat on Liberation of Labour Street, in one of the solid blocks built under Stalin with fat stucco cornucopias on the mustard-coloured facade. Inside the flat, there was little trace of the Soviet years. Photographs of the Uvarovs' illustrious ancestors and the grandfather who had emigrated were propped on every surface. In the sitting room a grand piano stood open with a book of nineteenth-century ballads on the stand, and a bust of Plato gazed at the wall.

Mrs Uvarov appeared, a fragile, vivacious woman. 'Come into the kitchen. We'll have tea.'

We took our shoes off and sat down at the kitchen table while Mrs Uvarov summoned her daughters. 'Masha, Valya,' she trilled. 'Edik is here to tell us the gossip.'

Edik twined his large, bony legs together. 'Oh, Tatyana Mikhailovna, what can I say? Charlotte has cured my throat – you know how I suffer with it. Just one little pill – it's quite better.'

'No!' Mrs Uvarov began to lay out tea with jam on saucers, little meringues and sweets. 'Tell us, what was it? Of course we won't be able to buy it here, but my cousins in America, perhaps –'

'Oh, I don't – I can't think what the medical name is –'

'Well, you must be sure to let me know. Ah, here are the girls. What's kept you, girls?'

A pale, blonde girl hurried in, followed by her sister. 'Hello, I'm Masha,' said the first, smiling quickly. 'Edik told us all about you already . . . This is Valya.'

'Hi,' said Valya. At first glance, they were almost identical – there was probably less than a year between them. Yet everyone they met must have noticed how, by the injustice of nature, their faces differed. Where Masha's eyes were exhausted, Valya's were dark and luminous; Masha's unhealthy pallor was Valya's translucent complexion, while Masha's animated, nervous manner only emphasised her sister's look of passive fury.

'Oh, how delightful it is to have a foreigner here,' continued their mother brightly. 'You cannot imagine how we suffer in Voronezh, so isolated, not a cultured person in the whole city, is there, girls? How we long for news. Tell me, is it the fashion in Britain to look so scruffy?'

'Er . . . perhaps not.'

'Isn't it true,' asked Valya idly, 'that when foreigners come to Voronezh, they deliberately dress like tramps? They think that way they'll fit in?'

'No, I don't think so –'

'Don't mind Valya, she's in a mood,' interrupted Masha. 'Now Charlotte, tell us: are there other charming English students here? Will you bring them to meet us?'

'She means boys,' supplied Edik.

'Oh, Edik, shhh . . . of course I mean no such thing. We are all lovers of foggy Albion, you know, we've read all your literature –'

There was a slight pause. Then Valya yawned. 'You must understand. The point is that we can't leave this place.'

That autumn, after several years of worry and expense, Edik was registered as 'Idiot: Grade Three'. I bumped into him on Friedrich Engels Street as he returned from a final medical examination and he showed me his new identity card. 'Come and celebrate,' he said, grinning. 'My mother is at home frying eggs.'

The Grade Three Idiot in the Soviet system received various benefits: cheap fares on public transport, food and medicine coupons and, on occasion, special housing. I suspected, however, that the sums that had exchanged hands over Edik's file more than outweighed the economic benefits of idiocy. No, the real point was that idiots did not do military service. (Or not below the rank of General, as the Soviet joke went.)

And whereas grades One and Two might be subject to spells in psychiatric wards and unspecified doses of drugs, Three was more or less left to his own devices. For a time it had looked as if Edik would go down with a Two – all the Threes had gone for this year, according to the doctor – which would have been a little sticky, but still worth it, apparently. But at the last moment, Edik's dad managed to rustle up a few hundred extra, and the Three had come through after all. It was just in time – by some sleight of hand, Edik had avoided the army before university, and while he was a student he was safe. But now he had finished his degree, and the recruitment officers were circling.

Edik's mother, Polina Eduardovna, opened the door. Her hair was spun into a vast orange confection for the occasion. 'Edichka!' she hugged him. 'My little boy shall stay at home.'

Edik was at least two foot taller than his mother, but her thick black brow and gold-toothed grin were the visual expressions of a personality that towered over his. She whisked him about the hall in a stiff and jolly little waltz and sang 'Edichka, Edichka, Edichka of mine, in the garden a little berry, a little raspberry of mine!' until she ran out of breath and came to a stop, laughing.

Edik looked reproachfully at both of us and said, 'Shhh.'

'Now, Edik,' said Polina Eduardovna, pulling herself together, 'run out to the Gastronom and ask Maria Aleksandrovna for some sausage. Don't be long . . .'

The Gastronom was just opposite, an echoing hall with counters displaying tins of pilchards. The meat department stood empty; behind it a stocky blonde picked her teeth.

'Be so kind,' said Edik, 'as to tell us where we might find Maria Aleksandrovna, young lady.'

The blonde jerked her head backwards and inspected some small object she'd retrieved from a molar.

'Do please be so charming as to inform her that Polina Eduardovna sent me to see her. I believe she is expecting us.'

For some moments the blonde watched the object closely; then she popped it back into her mouth. She sighed, pushing herself off the counter with a thrust of her muscly behind, and disappeared into the cavernous storerooms out the back.

The Zelyony family, you see, had connections. Polina Eduardovna's acquaintances numbered bureaucrats and psychiatrists, the manager of the Gastronom and a lady who worked behind the shoe counter in the Univermag department store. Other acquaintances supplied car parts and petrol, medicines and travel permits. In the Aeroflot office they greeted Edik by name, and every month or so he paid a visit to the railway station, where the signal controller would be keeping a parcel for him from his cousins in Moscow.

Maria Aleksandrovna appeared, large and stern, and beckoned to us to follow her. Everyone knew what went on in the back of the shop – the stores stuffed with rare milk products, the stacks of fruit jellies and Birds' Milk cakes, the haunches of meat, all sold 'on the left' to fortunate and wily folk such as the Zelyonys. The latter were admired as often as resented. Everyone was fixing 'on the left' a little – but some were more talented at it than others.

'How is your mother keeping?' inquired Maria Aleksandrovna, leading us into an office that smelt of raw meat.

'She's well, thank you.'

'And I hear we must congratulate you?'

'Oh, yes . . .'

'A little idiot!' She glanced skittishly at Edik and pressed a string of pallid sausages into his arms.

Edik blushed. 'Thank you, Maria Aleksandrovna.'

He was quiet on the way back, holding the sausages away from his body with a look of disgust. Abroad, his look seemed to say, surely no one needs to suffer this humiliation to buy a kilo of horsemeat. Only in Russia does one have to be publicly branded an imbecile to get by. 'You see the kind of society one mixes with in Voronezh,' he said after a while, summoning up a laugh. 'You cannot call it civilised.'

Polina Eduardovna laid a table in Edik's room with cheese and salami and all sorts of delicacies, followed by a plate of sausages and slithery, steaming fried eggs. She refused to eat with us, laughing and smoothing her nice stout stomach. 'I must think of my figure!' Then she left us, only popping her head back in to say to me, 'Charlotte, Edik tells me you have a miraculous cure for his throat. You will tell me what it is, won't you?'

We ate and drank champagne until we were pop-eyed and rosy. Even Edik's pallor lifted, aided by the red shirt that he had changed into for the occasion. Then he put a finger to his lips, and took a large volume of Steinbeck from the shelves. 'Hidden from my father,' he hissed, pulling out a bottle of clear liquid from behind. 'My aunt distils it herself, from beetroot. Here's to the army, may they rot!'

We each drank a shot of the *samogon* and winced.

'It's good for you. My mother says it cleans the gut. Can you imagine what they would think in St Tropez if they were given a drink to clean the gut?'

'You're right. They don't have gut in St Tropez.'

Edik giggled. 'You know Valya has got rid of her boyfriend, the fat one? She might be going to America soon. They've got cousins there, of course.'

'But I thought she was in love!'

'It seems not. Mrs Uvarova is thrilled.' Edik thought for a minute and then brightened. 'Wait . . .'

He chose a record from the shelves. 'Latin America,' he said in parenthesis. He took up a fork from the table and put it between his teeth, as applause from the sixties crackled and died away. He adjusted his glasses, put one hand behind his head and pointed at the mirror with the other, giving himself a fiery look. Then he pulled me up from the sofa and, with a pointy-toed kick, the tango began.

Foreign travel became easier under perestroika. Business and cultural exchanges were funded by well-meaning organisations in the West, and the embassies in Moscow were swamped by Russians with invitations from long-lost relatives and friends. Several people we knew had been abroad – Sasha had spent a year at Atlanta University on a scholarship, Yuri had been invited to England by a friend.

The process was still tortuous, however, and the pitfalls were many. First you needed an external passport, a separate little red book to the internal passport that you were required to carry at all times. If you happened to have spent your military service in an area of restricted access – anything from telecommunications or tanks to nuclear submarines – then you could be refused a passport. Likewise if you had lived in a 'closed city', the scientific research city at Akademgorodok in Siberia, or cities that produced armaments, or the space city in Kazakhstan. Cosmonauts, for instance, could easily have been refused a passport to travel to Germany. The local KGB openly took an interest in your plans to travel; around this time, a friend was sent an invitation in the post by an English girl. It never arrived; instead his father got a call from an officer of the KGB one day. 'We've got an invitation here for your son from an *anglichanka*. What do you know about that?'

The invitation was the second step. An invitation from a British business, stating that they'd pay for their Russian guest, more or less guaranteed a visa. It was the same for British travellers hoping to visit Russia, except that in London you can simply buy an invitation from a travel agency. Many times I've queued at the Russian embassy clutching a letter from, say, a language school in Ryazan, or from the Yaroslavl Institute of Forestry demanding my presence for a New Year conference; in some dusty file I must have an alternative career as professional negotiator and conference participant.

For most Russians this route was not possible. The next step for them was to try with a personal invitation, although these applications were always met with suspicion. Somehow the Home Office had boundless faith in the benefits of business travel, no matter how unsavoury the trade that it generated (and some of it really was unsavoury: during 1991, for example, two Chechens travelled to London to arrange an arms deal; they were murdered in their rented flat and smuggled out in a freezer by their Armenian assassins). This faith was matched, however, by their distrust of invitations from friends, and above all friends of the opposite sex. The KGB and the Home Office, just like Mrs Uvarova, concentrated on averting the disaster that any one of these personal invitations concealed – the Unsuitable Marriage.

Edik had no problem with his external passport – his mother saw to that – but he did not have an invitation. He never asked me for one – even if it wasn't for the drawback of an invitation from a girl, he was much too diffident to ask – and no one, including me, offered. The others took a different view of his Chekhovian tendencies – pretentious, they called them – and somehow my patience ran out too. I grew irritable, while Edik indulged his talent for subtle insult.

'Why is it that your country sends us only junk?' he'd say when I brought his mother a Mars bar.

'For someone like me, it is very hard to talk to uncultured people. It gives me a physical pain, in the kidneys – my kidneys are very sensitive,' he'd announce loudly at our parties.

And after I met Mitya, he'd shake his head and say sorrowfully, 'Poor Charlotte. She has been spoilt by that vulgar boy.'

Yet he was not to be thwarted. At the beginning of winter he went to Moscow to stay with the aunt he'd been counting on, a cheerful lady who had been widowed twenty years before and recently had found love with a chubby Pole. While she was in Krakow, Edik stayed in her flat, crammed in between her belongings: nineteenth-century armoires stuffed with dried fish and old newspapers, pickle jars and plastic bags. The whole was coated with an inch of greasy dust that made Edik smell like an old man. He returned to Voronezh at weekends to be fed and washed by his mother, and to boast about the big city.

'It's quite true what they say about Moscow being just a big village,' he'd say airily. On Edik's lips there were few worse insults. 'A huge, filthy village! But you know I see it as a stepping stone.'

So it was that quite soon he came to visit us in the hostel. He hummed and giggled; he obviously had something to tell us.

'How's things, Edik?'

'Oh fine, fine . . . I've got a lot to do organising my visa,' he said, studying his nails.

'Where to, Edik?'

'Well, I've had a job offer –'

'You're going abroad!'

'Yes, as a matter of fact, I've got a job in the leisure industry in Malta – at the Royal Malta Hotel.'

Edik's preparations were elaborate. He fussed about his suitcase, his English, his clothes. He visited everyone to ask if there was anything they needed from the West, a kindness which was misinterpreted by some who took pleasure in thinking up the most implausible and complicated errands: 'My mother asks if you could bring her a tin of Maltese grapes, for her lumbago.' 'My great-great-uncle was a Knight of the Cross – find out about my inheritance, would you, Edik?'

There was a party for him in the hostel the evening that he left. He perched on the edge of a bed, clearly in a state of wild excitement, though he sighed wearily when Viktor opened another bottle of vodka and said, 'How uncouth. In Malta they won't believe me when I describe it . . .' Poor Edik. Even on this triumphant day, we couldn't resist teasing him.

'So tell us about Malta, Edik.'

'Well, it's an ancient Mediterranean civilisation, very cosmopolitan . . .'

'What's the population of Malta, Edik?' someone asked in a casual voice. 'About five hundred thousand, isn't it?'

'Five hundred thousand!' someone else spluttered. 'But that's half the population of Voronezh. About the same number as live on the left bank!'

There was a pause and everyone started laughing.

'Don't be silly,' said Edik sniffily. 'It's quality, not quantity.'

But someone sang, 'Leaving the small town, heading for the bright lights –' which made us laugh even more. Eyes were wiped and beds were thumped. Still giggling, we accompanied Edik to the station, sliding over the slushy platform, installing him in his *coupé* to Moscow. We kissed him and gave him one last shot of vodka (so he'd sleep well), and waved goodbye to his pale, tense face framed by the train window with its two little embroidered curtains. And when the big green train had finally lumbered out of the station, someone said, 'Well, there he goes, off to civilisation,' and we were forced to sit down on a nearby bench and stamp our feet to gain control of ourselves. Viktor pinched himself so hard he had a bruise for a week. But the girls weren't allowed to sit for long, because the cold is a danger to the ovaries, and so we returned to the hostel.

Much later, Edik described his stay in Malta to me. Coming out of the airport building on a late autumn day, he was astonished by the heat. In Moscow it had snowed some weeks before; here it was still late summer. He took a gulp of salty Maltese air and thought to himself simply, I've made it.

The hotel had sent a car for him, driven by a laconic character who did not respond to Edik's attempts at conversation. So Edik sat quietly in his new cream mac with his briefcase tucked under his feet, and relaxed for the first time since he'd left Voronezh. Before they had left the urban sprawl that enclosed the airport, he was asleep.

When he woke more than an hour later, they were still winding their way through industrial estates, roundabouts and half-built tower blocks. 'Almost there,' said the driver finally, turning down a brand new road. They drove under a ranch-style gate, proclaiming 'Majestic Tourist Complex'. On the right was an area of waste ground pegged out with orange twine; up ahead a digger swivelled, depositing sand beside a concrete structure. The driver swerved around a pile of building materials and accelerated towards a white block with a sign: the Royal Malta Hotel. Here Edik had been employed as a night porter.

The next afternoon, a coachload of off-season holidaymakers arrived. Edik watched as they spilled rowdily into the foyer to be issued their room keys and a list of rules: 'It is forbidden to consume alcohol in the lifts and corridors. Guests are responsible for clearing up their own vomit. Any damage to room fittings is not covered by the package and must be paid for separately . . .' He went and changed into his hotel uniform – a cheap white shirt and black polyester trousers – and looked at himself in the mirror. After a moment's thought, he took out a small, sky-blue silk scarf and tied it around his neck, tucking it under his collar. Then he took up his post in reception.

For a month he watched drunken tourists retching into the ornamental fountain. They'd been promised sun and sea, but of course at that time of year there was not enough of the first and too much of the second, and the drinking took on a reckless edge. They thought Edik was hilarious. When he spoke his careful English to them, they hooted. The more generous gave him tips which made him blush. In his time off, he wandered through the souvenir shops and sunbathed when he could, although it gave him a rash. Needless to say, he never found tinned Maltese grapes, nor the mythical inheritance. Nor did he find the civilisation he was looking for.

When he returned, it was some time before we heard from him. His aunt returned from Kracow with her Pole, and there was no room for Edik in her flat. He came back to Voronezh and worked for a few weeks on an EU project, interpreting for two Germans, although he complained about them, saying, 'The Germans have a problem with taste.' Then, without saying goodbye, he disappeared to Moscow to stay with another cousin.

It was already spring the next time I saw Edik. He was picking his way though the slush in the streets, wearing imported spectacles and the blue overcoat of an international financier. He had an air of having returned from a better world.

'My God, Edik, look at you!' I exclaimed.

But he pretended not to know what I was talking about, saying only, 'How scrawny you've become. You look terrible! Come and see the Uvarovs this evening, we'll feed you up.'

Edik hadn't lost his way with words. Yet at half past six Emily and I were at the Uvarovs' door, holding a cake called Occasion and a bottle of Cagor, the communion wine, which stained the glasses purple. It was considered rather a delicacy in Voronezh.

'*Entrez*, girls!' Mrs Uvarov said, throwing the door open. 'It's Paris in here tonight. Edichka has come fresh from Paris two days ago, he's brought it all with him.'

'Paris? What was he doing there?'

'Oh, you know he's working for a bank now, they sent him on a business trip. Don't ask me what he does there, it's far too complicated for me. Sit down, girls, it'll be ready in a minute.'

In the sitting room the large round table, covered with a white cloth, was piled with Parisian *gourmandise*. There were plates of charcuterie and cheeses, and, in the centre, a tin of foie gras on a plate of ice. On a side table stood four bottles of glistening French champagne. I slid our bottle of Cagor behind the other bottles, out of sight. Edik was obviously doing well for himself at the bank.

At last Valya and Masha brought in the last dishes and Edik's mother announced, 'It's time to start. Sit down, everyone, let's begin.' She plumped down next to me, touching my shoulder kindly. The Uvarov parents sat next to Emily, the sisters next to them, in front of the piano; the seat beside the bust of Plato awaited its occupant. At last Edik appeared; he stood for a minute with one hand on Plato's head and surveyed the table with a restrained smile. He was wearing a dark blue suit, with a trouser crease that detracted just once from the vertical, near the shoe. Underneath the jacket was a white shirt and a sky-blue silk tie that fell in one voluptuous fold before vanishing into a waistcoat, buttoned rather high. 'Well, eat up,' he said. 'Of course none of this French stuff can really compare with good Russian produce . . .'

As we exclaimed and toasted, polished our plates with bread and filled them up again, moved on to vodka and helped ourselves to a little more cheese, it occurred to me that Edik had switched roles since I first met him. In fact he had moved into a different play. Chekhovian characters don't go to Moscow, certainly don't return dapper and prosperous. No, this Edik came as the rich uncle in a comedy – not a Russian play at all, a story in some pleasant French market town. Next to him sat the sisters, Masha inclining her head towards him, Valya glowering. The two mothers gossiped together, rolling their eyes at Edik – they were making a plan. Mr Uvarov, crushed by long exclusion, was trying to put in a few practical queries – length of flight, cost of Parisian Métro – but Edik was halfway through telling the girls a story. I heard him say '. . . and they saw *Idiot* on my passport, and let me straight through! I didn't declare a thing!' A burst of laughter swamped all talk; Edik's mother roared, clutching her bosom, Masha flung her head back, even Valya giggled. In the centre, Edik beamed. He loosened his sky-blue tie and unbuttoned his waistcoat, puffing out his stomach. He was right. A bit of weight would suit his new persona.

A few days later, Edik described his first day in Paris to me, and it became clear as he talked that his happiness, as far as it could be pinpointed, began with the purchase of that beautiful suit. He was not met at the airport on this trip. He arrived at Charles de Gaulle in the early morning and thought at first he would go to his hotel and have some breakfast. But when he stepped off the bus in the centre, onto a cobbled street full of Parisians behaving exactly as he hoped Parisians would – café owners sweeping the pavement, boys running with baguettes, old ladies walking small dogs – he began to explore. Soon he found himself on a wide avenue – the Champs Elysées.

Edik walked faster. There was a particular shop he planned to visit near here, a destination, the very wellspring of bourgeois medicine. He asked directions of a smart, middle-aged lady.

'Yves St Laurent? Just down that street there,' she answered, looking him up and down.

The doors of Yves St Laurent rotated silently and Edik entered a large, hot, minimally decorated shop; two assistants approached him, unsmiling, from opposite corners, to ask if assistance was what he required, or perhaps something else. And Edik took a breath, gestured to himself from head to toe, and uttered the two words he had prepared.

'Dress me,' he said.

5

The Triangle Player

I once believed that
Books are made like this:
Along comes a poet
Gently unlocks his lips and
The simple soul at once bursts forth in song.
God save us!
But it seems in fact
Before they sing
They tramp for days, restlessly rubbing up
blisters . . .

Vladimir Mayakovsky,
'A Cloud in Trousers', 1915

In October, a boy I had not seen before appeared in the corridor. He was drawing fiercely on the last of a cigarette, and I noticed a scar in the shadow of one of his cheekbones. He started to talk about Hitchcock; we disagreed about one of his films, I forget which.

'Come and watch *Psycho* with me tonight,' he said suddenly.

'No thanks. I *hated* that film.' I realised as the words came out that I'd never even seen it.

'Oh,' said the boy. 'OK.'

'I mean . . . For some reason, I just –'

'Hated it,' he supplied. 'Well, see you around then.'

When he had disappeared down the stairs, I asked Ira who he was. 'Oh, that's Mitya,' she said. 'Good-looking, isn't he?'

Half an hour later, I dropped in on the Uvarovs on the way to the market. Mrs Uvarov and Masha were cooking a stew for Mr Uvarov's birthday, standing over it and filling it with wishes. 'Come in, Charlottochka, come in. Now you can stir with us . . . I've asked for a distinction in my exams and the sweetest little pair of red boots I saw on Ulyanovskaya. Mama's asked to be able to get into her black dress.' Masha pushed the spoon into my hand, but when I shut my eyes I could only think of the ridiculous way I'd talked to that boy.

'So, what did you wish?' they asked together.

'Oh – in England we think that if you say your wish out loud, it won't come true –'

'No!' Mrs Uvarov looked horrified. 'Then what shall I wear for our dinner?'

'Tell us what you wished for, Charlotte,' said Masha. 'Or perhaps I should say who?'

'Oh, nothing like that . . . I wished for – strawberries.'

'Strawberries!' they squawked in unison. 'But it's October!'

A still, bright autumn had given way to the unsettled weather that heralded winter. For a week, the city lay under low cloud; it rained, then blew. In a few of the wooden houses down by

the river, they still followed the old-fashioned practice of seal-
ing the windows for winter: refitting the double glazing which
had been taken out in spring, cramming rags into the cracks.
In the hostel, they cranked the heating up another five
degrees; we flung the windows open and wore T-shirts. Gusts
of tepid air blew tatters of plastic across the hostel entrance,
stopped, then swept them back again.

Everyone is affected by the changes of season in Russia.
You feel a little anxious, and yet a general lassitude prevents
you from identifying the cause; you are irritable and yawning,
but alert to the smallest sounds, which seem unbearably rep-
etitious. One afternoon I fell asleep and woke just as the light
was going. Ira and Joe were dozing on Ira's bed, and for once
the corridor was quiet. Something had altered. I opened the
fortochka and felt it: a cold, steady wind blowing from the east.
The Russian winter was on the move.

'Oh, what a draught,' murmured Ira, stirring. 'It'll snow
soon.' She sat up, wrapping her dressing gown more closely
about herself. Joe slept on. 'I saw Mitya in class. He said
he'd been at a friend's dacha last week, only thirty kilometres
out of town, and snow had fallen in the night.'

I shivered.

'Are you cold? Shut the window, would you? We'll have flu
by evening otherwise.' Ira got up and opened the fridge. 'He
asked after you.'

'What did he say?'

'Oh, nothing much.'

'Ira –'

There was a laugh in her voice. 'He said, How's Charlotte? And I said, Fine . . . He says he's going to drop in.'

It isn't only me, I'm sure, that associates the arrival of winter with impatience.

The first time Mitya and I went out, we got tickets to a reading by Garkusha, punk poet, dancer and something of a cult figure for young Russians. Wet early snow had been blown in on the east wind the day before, hardly settling on the ground, but picking out the city in white. It coated the east-facing sides of trees and buildings, the 3-D lettering above the shops, and one of Peter the Great's rotund cheeks.

The yard outside the theatre was packed with boys hoping for spare tickets. They were in their best gear, smoking *papirosy*, Russian cigarettes with a long tube of cardboard for a filter. Most of them were no older than sixteen. Slouched against the walls and chewing on their cigarettes, deadpan as cowboys, they looked adorable. We squeezed past them and into an auditorium wedged solid with people.

'Over to the left,' Mitya said in my ear. He took my hand and pulled me over to a corner where two guys were leaning against the wall and rolling a joint. '*Privyet*, Lapochka, how's life? Hello, Horse.'

They shook hands and the Horse looked up from the joint and grinned. He had a strange, knobbly head, hairless apart from a little blond fur in places, bulging brown eyes, a nose like a potato on the end of a stick, ears that seemed to have gone to seed, and a smile of great charm.

'A gift for Garkusha,' uttered the Horse, gesturing at the joint, and Lapochka laughed and waved his arms about, as far as he was able in the crush. He was small and excitable, dressed in a ragged suit.

'There's nothing so educational as good grass. Re-education of the people is our aim. In the great struggle for the enlightenment of the people, we shall be tireless,' he gabbled.

'Et cetera,' spoke the Horse.

'Precisely,' agreed Lapochka. 'Et cetera, and so on.'

Garkusha entered and the hall went off like an alarm clock. A gangly figure in white, he stood in the centre of the stage looking vaguely about him. Flowers landed at his feet, followed by a bucket. There was a surge from the back that knocked all the air out of me; a lad behind was yelling *Gark*—! A familiar figure appeared on the stage – the Horse, who gave Garkusha the joint and loped off again. The crowd exploded with joy. Garkusha, tucking the gift behind his ear, pulled a pile of tiny pieces of paper from his pocket and began to read his poems.

I was finding it hard to concentrate on the performance. Mitya and I were squashed so close together, his face was no more than six inches away from mine. As the crowd surged against us, I was acutely aware of his arm around my back, holding me away from the flailing arms behind. He turned towards me and for a second I thought he was going to kiss me. Instead he just said, 'Shall we leave?'

I blushed. 'OK. I can't hear a thing.'

The cold made me gasp as we left the building. The temperature had dropped and outside the theatre the snow, half-melted and then frozen, drooped and swagged from the railings like icing. Lacy frou-frou dressed the statues and the trees. Mitya and I fell silent. It was as though we had stepped into the set of a musical, the still air humming with romantic expectation. We both spoke at the same time, and stopped.

'Well –' Mitya started again. 'Perhaps tomorrow we'll go somewhere where there's less of a crowd?'

I laughed, relieved. At the hostel the *vakhtersha* – the concierge – refused to let Mitya further than the hall. We shared a cigarette on the doorstep and then said goodbye awkwardly. He thrust his hands into his pockets and hunched his shoulders against the cold. I watched him until he rounded the corner, a dark figure against the bluish, snowy light.

It was impossible to be alone in the hostel. In our room, at any time of the day, Ira and Joe would be dozing, friends popping in and out, and there'd be a stream of queries at the door – Could we borrow a frying pan? A teaspoon? Five hundred roubles? Out in the corridor people were changing money, drinking, having crises of one sort or another.

Where else, then? Not Mitya's flat: his mother, father, brother, dog and parrot would be bursting with friendly curiosity. There were no bars, and the neon-lit ice-cream parlours were not inviting. The only place to be private was out in the open. At night, the ill-lit, potholed back streets were empty; only the occasional figure hurried along, buttoned into his overcoat, thinking of home. There was little traffic, and the sound of televisions turned up loud in the apartments that we passed only added to the sense of intimacy.

Most evenings, Mitya and I met by the Cinema of the Young Spectator. When I stepped off the trolley bus he'd be waiting, always smoking, beneath the huge hand-painted billboard. His eyes seemed to close entirely when he smiled. '*Nu-ka, posmotrim*, let's have a look,' he'd say, fussing over my scarf. Winter had begun in earnest since we'd met. The snow that gleamed in the long stretches between street lights would now lie until spring, and the thermometer hovered around five degrees below – nothing severe, like the plummets into double figures still to come in December and January, but enough to convince Mitya that I was dangerously incompetent at dressing for the cold. I confess it was a moment I enjoyed: Mitya, smoking with no hands and narrowing his eyes like a private detective as he tightened the toggles on my coat.

Then we'd set off, walking fast to keep warm. This was how I discovered the city – in the half-dark, taking short cuts through patches of waste ground and around the unfinished Party building, whose construction had come to a halt suddenly when perestroika began. The shops looked glamorous at night, lit by sparkling chandeliers, gilded, and full of *recherché* goods that I never saw at other times. One day I bought a furry green bowler hat, another a pair of leather ice skates. The evening we emerged from a shop, giggling, with a white periwig in a box, Mitya pulled me into a doorway and kissed me in the darkness.

Certain places we returned to and made our own. We drank beer on the hot-water pipes outside one of the few nineteenth-century merchant's houses in Voronezh. Up by the church was a statue in the Soviet monumental style; we huddled in the shelter of its billowing greatcoat and gazed over the reservoir to the industrial sector on the left bank, which glittered like Manhattan. The statue had begun life as Stalin, but just as they put the finishing touches to it, Khrushchev made his speech condemning the 'cult of personality'. So the municipal council whipped Stalin's head off and substituted the head of Koltsov, a local poet noted for his love of nature.

Mitya liked that sort of thing. When we approached his favourite places – the statues in the Children's Park, for instance, masterpieces of Soviet kitsch, or the place by the railway station where a heap of two-foot-tall steel letters spelling 'All hail to the Communist Party of the USSR!' lay rusting in a heap – he'd take larger and larger steps and start waving his arms. 'Look!' he'd shout. 'Isn't that wonderful!'

As we walked, we built up a collection of stories that became so closely associated with real places that they were as good as true. I can't remember what provoked the idea that one of the trolley buses – you couldn't tell which one – was the random bus, which took you to a random destination. Occasionally we'd see people on the street who, we swore, had just got off the random bus. They had that lost look. We grew to be so superstitious about this that quite often we let buses go by that we considered had something sinister about them. Babushkas knew which were the evil ones, we thought.

If there were two or three old ladies waiting with their elbows out, ready to scurry on board, it was probably safe. It was really nothing more than an excuse to stay out later.

Late each evening Mitya's silhouette disappeared around the corner and I turned back to the hostel, which wore an air of post-coital smugness that almost drove me mad. Ira and Joe would be dozing peaceably together in our room. Emily and Yuri were down in Room 99, partying. Yakov and Nina were still going out together: it seemed as though every time you opened a cupboard, they would appear out of it, looking rumpled and dusty and pleased. Why were Mitya and I incapable of doing the same? We were bashful, that was all, and awkward. Out in the street it all came naturally, but indoors I was always flinging my arms up and almost breaking Mitya's nose, and then he'd tread on my toes, and we'd both get embarrassed. It was not lack of willingness; I'd have gone into a cupboard with Mitya any day, though it's lucky, with hindsight, that we didn't. We'd probably have done each other permanent damage. As it was we walked until our feet were frozen and our noses turned from red to purplish-grey. We walked and walked and still slept badly at nights.

At a certain point it became too cold to stay outside all evening. There was a crazed feeling about the hostel: the siege was beginning. It was October, and we'd be in this together until April at the earliest. There was a lot of drinking and Sasha, who had been in Afghanistan, went on a three-day bender and smashed his room up.

Ira and Joe didn't care – they lay motionless and gazed into each other's eyes. Twenty people could be dancing in their boots so the floor bounced and plaster dust streamed on top of them, and Joe's beatific smile would not waver. It has to be said that large amounts of drugs played a part in this admirable repose. Mitya and I couldn't emulate it: we just wanted to be on our own.

Soviet culture came unexpectedly to our aid. In Voronezh there were at least three cinemas, as well as the Opera theatre, the Philharmonia, the puppet theatre, the Theatre of the Young Spectator and the Drama theatre. Mitya and I saw every show in town. We went to double bills at the cinema on Revolution Prospect, and to hear Gershwin played in the afternoons at the Philharmonia. We began to recognise the musicians: the patrician oboist with his hair slicked back, and the first violinist who seemed always on the verge of tears. The audience, too, repeated itself – four or five old ladies who never missed a concert, a large self-satisfied man who announced his opinion: 'Of course they do not understand Gershwin, not at all.'

We sat at the back and dreamt, and Mitya leant over and whispered in my ear. 'One day we'll live on a yacht. Thousands of kilometres of empty sea on every side.'

Our venue of choice, however, was the Opera. The theatre itself, like a bulky old dowager with her jewels on, had a particular charm. A row of fat, stumpy columns adorned the façade, while inside the hall was marble, lit by grimy chandeliers. The theatrical terms in Russified French sounded to me genteel in the extreme.

'You're sitting in the *parterre*,' we were told. 'There will be one *entrakt* of twenty minutes.'

Tickets for the front row of the stalls cost six roubles (about fifteen pence), and there was a specially shaped brass plate at the box office to receive your coins, and an old women in the *garderob*, the cloakroom, who told me off every time we came for not having sewed a hook into my coat.

It was a repertory theatre and the productions had been doing solid service for years. Part of the enjoyment came from the fact that age had not so much added its patina as scraped off the polish. These were no seamless, flawless creations: the performers wrestled visibly with their roles. They sweated, they heaved, they suffered in too-tight corsets. And the audience rewarded them for it. They applauded the physical feats, the arias belted out against all the constraints of costume, the rickety staircases managed at a run, the sword fights that ended in panting corpses. Mitya and I saw every detail from our front-row seats.

It was at the Opera that we first saw the triangle player. During an uneventful performance of *Evgeny Onegin*, we found our attention distracted by the orchestra. There were some of our friends from the Philharmonia again. But about half an hour into the first act, the pit door opened and in strolled a young man with an instrument case. He sat down, took a novel out of his pocket, and began to read. After a few minutes he searched about in his pocket and found a boiled sweet. We were so close that a waft of sickly orange reached us. The conductor, we thought, looked agitated. After some time, the young man stirred. Still reading, he reached out with one hand to open the instrument case and take out his triangle. He stood up and asked the drummer next door to show him where they'd got to. For half a minute or so he waited, then struck a little ping-a-ling-a-ling. Then, to our great delight, he packed up his triangle and his book, nodded goodbye to his neighbour, and left.

After the interval Mitya and I couldn't bring ourselves to watch the rest of Tatyana's fate. Instead we sat in the Opera buffet, well known for its Turkish coffee and *zefir*, nutty meringues, and revelled in the idea of the triangle player.

'He's probably been working up to that position for years,' said Mitya. 'First in the youth orchestra, then as understudy . . .'

I giggled. 'Years. He must dream of triangles . . .'

'Yes – street signs, and geometrical bosoms, and the secrets of the Great Pyramid . . .'

'And what about his home life? He practises so much, his triangle comes between him and his wife, and one day he finds her in bed with the conductor.'

When we had eaten as many meringues as we could we walked back to the hostel, planning a crime novel around our hero. Three lovers, three deaths, and the most unbearable suspense until the last page, when, with a single ping!, it would be revealed that . . .

At the hostel the *vakhtersha* as usual made trouble and would only let Mitya in for half an hour. We stood on the steps for a bit and then Mitya went home, as always, digging his hands deep into his pockets. I wanted to cry. The entire Soviet system seemed to be at the third point in our triangle.

It was the Uvarovs who unwittingly supplied the answer to our dilemma. At the end of October, Masha visited Emily and me in the hostel. She stood in our room trying not to notice the squalor, as though she had a favour to ask. In fact, the opposite was true: Masha took me aside and whispered that the whole family was going up to Moscow for the week, and perhaps we would like to borrow their flat? As I accepted, hurriedly, the fancy occurred to me that it was the wish that I had tossed into their stew, digested and become thought.

Emily and I moved into the flat on Saturday and marvelled at the luxury. It was not a lavish flat by most standards, but we had hot showers whenever we wanted and a clean cooker. Hell, we sat in separate rooms and couldn't *hear* each other – that felt good. I slept on a bed in the sitting room, in an alcove hung with red velvet curtains.

Mitya was out of town for most of the week at a wedding, and there was no way of letting him know the news. But on Friday he returned and rang to say that he was coming round, instantly, he was on his way.

Emily and Yuri had gone to Moscow the day before. Edik, Ira and Joe had been with me all afternoon drinking tea, but they grinned when they heard Mitya's voice and immediately stood up to go. Suddenly I was alone. I put on lipstick, wiped it off again and stared at myself in the mirror. I cleaned my teeth and instantly felt embarrassed at the idea that Mitya would notice the smell, so I drowned it with a glass of the Uvarovs' Armenian brandy, which tasted disgusting after toothpaste. In the mirror I caught sight of my grimace and laughed at myself. My pulse was racing, and I laughed at that too. I flung myself on the sofa to read, nonchalantly, but a second later sprang up again to make my bed.

Just as I'd pulled all the sheets back, Mitya arrived. He showed no signs of noticing the bed or the blush that burnt all the way down to my collarbones. He was covered in powdery snow, out of breath, saying 'Look!' He pulled back the curtains. 'Blizzard.'

Out of the darkness, snow was coming at the window, swirling past it on a vicious wind. Beyond it, we could see only the glimmer of a few streetlights wreathed by flakes. Nothing was still; it was like a storm at sea. As we watched, the lights all down the street went out. A power cut.

By candlelight, Mitya prepared Russian Bloody Marys. 'You pour the tomato juice in first,' he said. His hair, still a little damp, fell in two curls on his forehead. 'Then you take a knife and slide the vodka down it, slowly, so that it sits on top.' Around our table with its few candles the world seemed to have fallen quiet. The only movement was the snow, flying silently past us.

'It feels as though we are the two survivors of a disaster,' Mitya murmured.

'We'll have to stay in our bunker for twenty thousand years.'

'Exactly . . . how will we pass the time?'

I laughed. 'Oh, well – haven't we learnt to be patient by now?'

'Patient!' Mitya burst out. 'Only when we have to be. Come here –'

Much later, in the little bed with its red velvet curtains, Mitya looked at me slyly. 'We have a responsibility, after all,' he remarked, 'being the only survivors.'

'Mmm?'

'To refound the human race –'

'Oh God, I hadn't thought of that.'

The snow was pattering against the window. Mitya pulled the blankets up over us, over our heads. I could feel him smiling in the darkness. 'Although on the other hand,' he remarked, 'it's all right being on our own.'

At half past seven on Saturday morning I woke up. Mitya had left to go to classes, my head had been exchanged for a large blunt object, and I couldn't work out what that remote ringing sound meant. At last I realised: it was Mr and Mrs Uvarov pressing their own doorbell. They must have caught an earlier train. I grabbed my dressing gown and ran into the kitchen, kicking a brimming ashtray across the room. At midnight, seeing as the sink was already full, it had seemed a good idea to stack the dirty dishes on the floor. The tablecloth was covered in candle wax and tomato juice. I was just trying to stuff it into a bucket when the Uvarovs, giving up on me, opened the door with their key.

With one glance they took in my dressing gown, the state of the flat, the empty vodka bottle, and my frozen, guilty expression. They did not utter a single reproach, but Mrs Uvarov let out a tiny sigh. She was disappointed. Silently we tidied the flat and I left as soon as I could to go to classes. Our friendship never wholly recovered from this blow. Yet once I was out on the street, I couldn't stop myself from grinning and breaking into a run.

· 6 ·

Russian Lessons

Lesson I: Practice

On the first night we arrived in Moscow, back in September, a frenzy to speak to the nearest Russian took hold of me. We were crossing Paveletsky station, lit by neon strips that threw an inadequate, harsh glare. A great crowd was hurrying and jostling, breathing steam into the darkness and heaving too-heavy bundles. Packages, bedrolls, boxes were piled in corners, with little old women no bigger than dolls perched on top of them, looking fearfully from side to side. Young men smoked and kept guard. Women produced hard-boiled eggs from their handbags and fed their blank-eyed children. What was this great exodus? I had no way of finding out: all the Russian I'd ever known had vanished. Except for one word.

'Son,' I blurted out to the porter who was pulling a cart with our luggage on it. 'Do you have a son?'

He stopped and raised his eyebrows. 'Do I have a son?' he repeated indignantly. 'What difference is it to you?'

I blushed. 'None, nothing . . .'

He unloaded the bags, still annoyed. 'Son! What's that all about? Here I am struggling to make a living and they mock me with their questions.'

For some time my Russian produced unpredictable results. I learnt by ear, slipping words that I liked into sentences without quite knowing what they meant. The expression *naoborot* – 'on the contrary' – sounded to me the height of linguistic sophistication.

'How's things?' people would ask.

'On the contrary, very good,' I'd reply.

The few poems that I'd learnt in Russian were wheeled out again and again. Lermontov's meditation on a lonely white sail at sea supplied several useful phrases. For instance, when the windows in the bus were broken I could remark in beautiful Russian, 'The wind whistles, and the mast creaks and groans!' When a cockroach scuttled out of our room, I exclaimed wittily, 'Alas, he is not seeking happiness, nor is he fleeing from it.' When I was tired, there was Pushkin: 'It's time, my friend, it's time; my heart begs for peace.' Sometimes people were taken aback: their eyes popped as though a small pig had just quoted their national poet. They corrected me: 'No, no, that is by our Russian genius, A. S. Pushkin!' As though I'd uttered the sacred formulation by accident.

Slowly my vocabulary began to grow. I had already found that all theatrical terms in Russian are simply borrowed from French; soon I discovered that, just like the English, Russians like to give anything that's a bit fancy a French name. If you're talking about food, clothes, literature or lovemaking and you can conjure up a little Frussian then not only will you probably be understood, but you'll come across as having – how shall I put it? – a certain *savoir-faire*. German is useful if you want to discuss military matters, maps, cigarette holders or shipbuilding. English comes in handy for conversations about computers, business, finance and so on; also for hippie slang: *hair* means long flat greasy hair, *shoesy* means a fashionable pair of shoes, and, best of all, *beatly*, from the Beatles, describes something very, very cool.

I learnt to speak Russian as students do. I began to answer 'How's things?' with a laconic 'normal', and to sprinkle my speech with slang that had evolved so elaborately that I didn't recognise the obscenity at its core. I even picked up something of a Voronezh accent – a soft, guttural tone that sounded faintly Ukrainian. People began to look at me askance and ask if, perhaps, I was from Poland? Or could it be the Baltics? Because they speak oddly, a bit like you.

One day two old ladies tugged at my coat on the bus. 'What's that funny language you're talking at?' they demanded.

'English,' Emily and I said. 'We're from England.'

'Oh.' They eyed us suspiciously, and a moment later we heard them muttering to each other. 'They're not English girls, those two – they're just trying to fool us! Look at that one –'

pointing at Emily – 'she's got Belorussian eyes. They're from Belorussia, that's what.'

English people should not be riding around on buses in Voronezh, wearing tatty clothes and carrying trays of eggs from the Central Market. Nor, really, should they be speaking Russian, even with an English accent. In previous centuries Russian peasants had a simple rule of thumb: Russians spoke and all the rest were *nemtsi*, dumb people. *Nemets* has evolved to mean German, but there is still a sense that you are not really a proper foreigner if you speak Russian.

'Why do you want to speak our language?' people were always asking, looking at us with ill-concealed pity.

'It's a beautiful language.'

They were unconvinced. 'Of course it's a beautiful language. But books, music, you can read and listen to them back home in comfort. Why come here?'

'It's stimulating to live in another country –'

'What, our poverty? The chaos we're in now?'

I always fell back on my one, incontrovertible reason. 'My mother was Russian –'

'Ah,' they'd say, relaxing. 'Now we understand. It's in the blood . . . Emigrés never really settle. In that case, of course you speak Russian.'

A certainty which, as I struggled to make sense of Russian grammar, I found rather a comfort.

Our teachers were a disparate lot, with the particular exaggerations that teaching seems to encourage. V. P. Pavlov was meticulously dull, with a mouthful of blackened stumps that made it painful to watch him talk. He discussed etymology in Novoyaz, Soviet jargon: 'The socio-philosophical aspect of this development leads us to the extrapolation of historical trajectories –' He was utterly unaware of this habit, like the girl in the fairy tale who spewed forth toads and foul-smelling insects every time she opened her mouth.

A. S. Saltykov was tall, handsome, intelligent, and so overwhelmed by cynicism that every time he lifted his hand to scratch his head one could see him thinking, 'What's the point?' His lessons were fascinating, and yet I always had to force myself to go to them, knowing that the rest of the day would be shadowed by his despair. Yulia Antonovna, on the other hand, was romantic in a folksy, plaits-and-toenails fashion. She taught a class called 'Musical Phonetics'; for a couple of hours a week we'd gather round as she strummed on her guitar and taught us Russian folk songs. Everything with her was in the diminutive. 'Let's sing a dear little song,' she'd suggest. 'A tiny song in a chordlet of *fah*.'

The teacher from whom I learnt the most was Rita Yurievna, a brisk, cerise-lipped matron with a sense of humour. Under her guidance we picked our way through the tangled forests of the Russian lexicon, as beautiful and as dark, in her eyes, as the Russian character itself. It has always seemed to me that grammar exercises reveal the culture that they spring from. The French book I was taught from featured Madame Bertillon, an air hostess, who was on a diet. 'Mme Bertillon a perdu du poids!' it announced approvingly. The first Russian sentences I came across, on the other hand, were a mystery. 'Is this a table?' asked a cheerful young student, pointing at something out of the picture. '*Nyet*!' sang back another student. 'It is a bridge!' It seemed a strange mistake to make.

Rita Yurievna's examples were more elaborately surreal. We were taught to be precise about whether we had crawled around the swamp just once, or many times; if we were in the habit of flying deep into strange territory or if it had been merely a temporary aberration; and how to differentiate between a crowd of people running to their respective homes and all converging on our own. Each case demanded a specific, prefixed verb.

'You must understand,' said Rita Yurievna, 'that in Russian, verbs are not only about action. They are also about the experience. Think how different it feels if you walk down a street every morning of your life, and if you walk down it for the first and only time. It may be the same action, but it is another experience entirely.'

Lesson I: Exercises

(a) Enter a restaurant or a café. You will be shown this piece of typewritten card:

MENYU

A LA KART

Bifshteks	Salat	Kofe
Krokety	Kartofel 'fri'	Chai
Kotlety	Kartofelnoye 'pyure'	

Select your meal.

(b) Go into a 'Universalny Magazin'. In which department will you find the following?
   (i)   trikotazh
   (ii) bootsi
   (iii) bustgalter
   (*h* in English often becomes *g* in Russian)

(c) Match these words up to their meanings:
baraban	bell
kolokol	violin
skreepka	drum

   Many Russian words are onomatopoeic.

(d) A little more Russian vocabulary that you didn't know you knew:
   straus – ostrich; pasternak – parsnip; tolstoy – an archaic word for fat.

Lesson II

I learnt most of my Russian from Mitya, of course. Several days a week, Mitya fixed it so that his classes didn't start until ten, two hours after his parents had left for work and taken his brother to school. Two hours in an empty flat: Rita Yurievna didn't stand a chance. On those days I stumbled out of bed and dressed in the kitchen so as not to wake the others. The streetlights were still lit; I slid through the snow and the shadowy light to the bus stop. I always glanced down Peace Prospect to check by the station clock that I was not early; I didn't want to bump into Mitya's mother on the stairs. By eight o'clock she would have left her younger son at school and set off for her engineering firm, never suspecting that some foreign girl, trembling with cold and excitement, was banging on her steel door.

Those snowy mornings, I began to gain a sense of the language; its soft, sliding rhythms that seemed to follow a looping pattern of their own until you reached the noun at the end of the sentence. Mitya teased me with strings of participles.

'Hello, pink-cheeked, having-walked-through-the-cold-morning-air, still-sleepy-eyed girl,' he greeted me.

'Mitya –'

'Come in and taste the having-been-smelt-in-the-hallway coffee.'

Russian is malleable, and Russians love to manipulate it, to roll the words around their mouths, to distort them, to re-invent them. Colours, for example, can become verbs; verbs are transformed with prefixes and turned back into adjectives and nouns; neologisms are a part of everyday speech. It makes for a wonderfully suggestive language, a language of association and imagination. And somehow its soft-shoe shuffle, its twisted vowels that turn *e* into *ye*, *o* into *a*, and the network of agreements in each sentence that give the impression of internal rhymes, all give spoken Russian a particular sensuality.

'Learning Russian is like falling in love,' Rita Yurievna

remarked on one occasion, looking knowing. 'To fall in love: *vlyubit'sya*. You take the verb to love, *lyubit'*, and add the prefix *v-*, meaning in, into. Then make it reflexive, because it is happening to you, isn't it? Not to anyone else. No one else could be feeling like this! Lovers always think they are unique. Isn't it a beautiful word?'

Mitya and I drank coffee in his parents' flat and tried to talk. We made precarious progress. On the one hand, misunderstandings were common. The hostel obscenities that I introduced randomly into the conversation were obviously a little surprising, but that was nothing to the surreal impressions I sometimes took away from Mitya's conversation. On one occasion we went to an exhibition. Mitya glanced at each picture and said casually, 'Yes, I painted that one. And that one. Yes, that one too.'

'What do you mean?' I asked.

'I painted them. It didn't take long. I did it as a favour to Fyodorov.'

It was an exhibition of Fyodorov's work. For a moment, the thought that I was with a dangerous megalomaniac eclipsed most others. Then I realised: he had written the descriptions posted up underneath the pictures, not painted them. The same verb, *pisat'*, could be used to mean either.

I realised after a time that learning Russian was as much a matter of adapting my tone as accumulating vocabulary. Russians, for example, have none of the contorted, apologetic manner of the English. If you start out on 'Would you possibly be so kind as to help me, if you've got a moment, to point out where the post office might be?' any Russian who is not a bureaucrat or an official will look at you as though you are mad. After a time I learnt to ask simply, 'Where's the post office?' Equally, the Russian habit of saying in a commanding tone, 'Give me one cigarette!' soon stopped sounding rude. Both the tone and the sentiment behind it, which assumes that the cigarette-rich person will always share them with the poor, came to feel quite natural. I was becoming Russian, it seemed to me; and the happy, swift feeling of losing myself was part of the process. '*Nichevo,*' I responded airily when there were problems, shortages; when, back in England, I would have grumbled. All of that was important, it was all necessary, and none of it mattered a bit, it was nothing – *nichevo.* The only piece that I have come across that captures this sensation was written by a Madame Jarinstzov, in 1919:

'True, with us it is *nichevo* when people walk into the room without knocking; or come without invitation at any time for the simple reason that they wish to see you; or men get up from their seats and pace the room up and down in the heat of a discussion during the course of a meal; all this is certainly *nichevo,* because these points are but trifles to a Russian mind, and the Westerner may smile with disgust or condescension at the thought of such manners! . . . True, again, a Russian will fly down a long, steep hill in his sledge, cart or brougham, and will say '*nichevo!*' if the vehicle happens to go into the ditch at the bottom of the hill.

But in ninety-nine cases out of a hundred it would not do so, because rushing down a hill is a universally beloved thing, to which generations of horses have been used since the time when the Russian land first began to be. And if a driver did not rise in his seat, and let all the reins loose, and shout words of love and encouragement to them at the sight of a steep road downwards, the horses would think that something had gone unmistakably wrong.'

· 7 ·

The Truth Game

With large-scale privatisation to come, state officials and
deputies are using their positions to take the best pieces
of the pie . . .

Observer, 27 October 1991

The *vakhtersha* beckoned me over one day with a little mittened hand and passed me a note: parcel for collection, Post
Office number so-and-so. It was a building that I hadn't
noticed before, slightly set back from the road, windows filled
with the sinewy Busy Lizzie plants that Soviet state employees felt so tenderly towards. Inside it was empty. I waited and
tried to breathe shallowly. The air was dense with familiar
Soviet smells – damp wool, tobacco, old people – and over-
laying them all an earthy, half-sweet stink, possibly human,
that made the saliva run nauseously in my mouth.

After some minutes a rustling noise in the back rooms grew
louder and a babushka appeared, carrying a mug of tea with
a piece of black bread laid over it. Her bottom lip was
clamped tight over her top and she gave no sign of noticing
me. Having learnt a little about such situations, I said nothing.

Officials, including shop assistants, train conductors and post office workers, did not belong to the majority of Russians who liked a direct and honest approach. If you came straight out with even 'Excuse me! I've been waiting . . .' or 'Sorry to disturb you . . .' this type of babushka was liable to fly into a rage and ignore you for a full five minutes. Of course it depended on who you were: pensioners, in particular veterans of the Great Patriotic War, had special privileges. They would have let fly a spittle-beaded stream of abuse. Otherwise the best technique was simply to stand there looking polite, and when she finally glanced at you, to thrust the ticket forward with a gush of flattering entreaty. 'Please, comrade, be so kind, I have a parcel waiting here?' If she still looked unconvinced, you might try an emotional appeal: 'From far away in my home country, how I've been missing it!'

This time, however, there was no need. When she read my name on the ticket she threw her hands up. '*Slava Bogu*! Thank goodness you've come.'

She returned within a few seconds with a box and pushed it at me, forgetting even to stamp my receipt for her records. It was postmarked six weeks previously. It was also, clearly, the source of the filthy smell.

'Off you go, *dochka*. Take it, and good health to you!'

It felt faintly warm in my hands as I carried it back to the hostel. Mitya was in my room when I arrived. He stubbed out his cigarette and together we slit open the packing tape. The box gave off a faint hiss and a stink that made us fall back and cover our mouths. Even Joe stirred in his sleep.

'Jesus,' he muttered. 'Sorry, everyone.'

At the bottom of the box was a cellophane packet blown up like a balloon, containing a blackish, lumpy puddle.

'What is it?' whispered Mitya, awed.

'I don't know,' I whispered back. 'But six weeks ago, I think it might have been . . . camembert.'

This hunch turned out to be right. A friend had made up a parcel of delicacies that were hard to come by in Voronezh: chocolate, crisps, magazines, and – my favourite – a piece of camembert. Not, perhaps, the most practical cheese to send by post. Six weeks had seen it pass through some intense organic processes.

'But why did it have to sit there all that time?'

'That'll be the KGB, *ublyudki*,' said Mitya, lighting a cigarette hurriedly. 'Kept it there for all that time. They'd never seen French cheese before. Halfwits.'

It was a memorable introduction to the secret police: a smell so bad you could almost hear it howl.

I was inclined to treat the KGB more as rumour than reality, until they started leaving deliberate hints. For example, not only had the letter inside my parcel been opened and read, but someone had put a cup of coffee down on it. Our post was always erratic, but occasionally a letter was delayed by months rather than weeks and arrived with words underlined, or with mysterious red marks in the margin. Whoever made these seemed not to understand English very well – perhaps they had simply been given a list of key words to identify. A friend received a letter in which her mother described setting off on holiday: 'We had to wait for an hour at the bank to pick up our foreign currency, and another to get the visa, so rushed to the station and only just caught the train.' In a dusty little office somewhere in Voronezh, a guardian of the Soviet state's security had carefully underlined 'foreign currency', 'visa', 'station', and had passed it on to his superior to request further action. The letter took several months to arrive.

Then several friends in the hostel told us that they had been called in for questioning – a friendly chat, apparently, in their blank-faced office block on Plekhanov Street.

'So, how's life in the hostel?' the officer would ask. 'Are Ira and Joe still going out together? Are they getting on well? Emily and Yuri, they going to get married? Or not? Eh?'

It sounded implausible to me. Surely, in these times of economic crisis, even the KGB had to earn themselves a living. What was the sense in paying these pathetic juniors – Cinderellas in brown suits – to stay late at the office, copying out the reports of our student parties? On the other hand, of course, the thought of files marked with our names being filled with details of hostel life was wonderfully comical, not to say glamorous. Perhaps they would be forwarded to Moscow, where some smooth-cheeked colonel would tap my documents, gaze out of the window and mutter, 'Hmmm, Charlotte Hobson . . . she sounds interesting.' It added a piquancy to life to imagine a secret biographer at our backs. We felt we had to keep providing him with material.

Yet – and for the first time the comedy turned a little sour – who was passing on the information from the hostel? We assumed it was one of the duties of the *Komendant* to keep the security forces up to date. But that didn't stop the rumours about other people. Almost the day we arrived, somebody took us aside and whispered: see him over there? He's KGB. Don't trust him. One of the British girls seemed unerringly to fall in love with them: the stringy, scrawny one; the one with black hair and a face like a hatchet; the kindly, plump one – according to the gossip, all of them were KGB.

Mitya hated the whole business. 'Only a *sovok* would believe all that stuff,' he said. A *sovok*: someone who lived in the old Soviet way, fearful, credulous, boot-licking, deceitful. 'All that is irrelevant now.'

He was right, of course. And yet we couldn't help listening to the stories when they came round.

We had a party on what remained of my parcel. A brown-eyed Russian called Peanut brought a couple of American students, Bill and Leda. Leda was wild. She looked like a swan herself: a long, taut neck and white skin which seemed barely to conceal the movement of her bones. She had black hair and sharp red lips and when she entered a room, you could feel fear and excitement rising in all the men. The gossip in the hostel had nothing but admiration for her.

Bill, on the other hand, was a clean-cut, tidy boy who was lodging with Peanut's family. He did not touch alcohol or nicotine, was conscientious about hygiene, and insisted on respect for the American flag. After college, he told us, he wanted to join the army. It was just the sort of behaviour that set tongues wagging. Somebody – as usual, no one knew who'd said it first – suggested that Bill's army ambitions meant something more specific. Intelligence, they said. Look how cagey he is, doesn't drink. That's always suspicious. Before long the consensus was that he was CIA. There's always one, people said. Believe us, it's sure to be him. He's bright, he keeps in training. There was no end of evidence once you got to thinking about it.

The rumours did Bill no harm; on the contrary, he became an object of curiosity. Everyone invited him to their parties and tried to persuade him to accept a glass of vodka. Men encouraged him to talk about the US army. Girls sat on his lap and asked him questions, and Bill's scrubbed face took on the permanent, amiable smile of the popular guy. Leda was the only one with the power to remove it: with an arch of her eyebrows, she could confuse him. But she, too, was intrigued.

'Come on, guys –' Leda sat on my bed between Peanut and Bill, the two flatmates. She leaned over to fill the glasses around her, the line of her bare arm gleaming in the half-dark. 'Drink with me. To New York City, am I glad to leave that place.'

'You know I don't drink,' said Bill. His T-shirt showed his pectorals; sitting quietly, he looked helpless, his big pink hands turned upwards on his lap. Leda just flared her nostrils a fraction and laughed.

'Darling, we're not in Atlanta now. We're in Russia, we drink.'

Bill looked at her, embarrassed. 'Give me a break, wouldya?'

Peanut stepped in. 'OK, New York,' he repeated. 'To Brighton Beach, where all the Russians with any sense have gone already.'

'Brighton Beach!' we echoed, and drank.

That evening I found myself watching the three of them: Peanut, leaning across and whispering to Leda, making her laugh; Leda, eyes glittering, letting her hand rest on Bill's knee. Bill sat between them like a great clean baby and blushed as Leda teased him about his biceps.

'I like a man with an arm measurement the size of my waist,' she said. 'Let's see – can you raise a shot glass to your mouth, or will you let me help you?'

At last Bill gave in, as everyone knew he would, and accepted some vodka. Everyone does – it is almost impossible to resist the collective will of Russians urging you to drink. It soon becomes clear that it is simply self-centred of you to keep on refusing. How can you think of your work, your sleep, your liver when all your friends are ruining their careers and their health so much faster and more conclusively than you? What kind of a person keeps a clear head to observe his comrades drinking away their youth? You need alcohol inside you to bear it. What's more, even one sober guest leaves a chill in the air. How are the rest of us to expand and float away with this cold draught to deflate us? It's pure selfishness not to drink, and it was to Bill's credit that he understood this and began, slowly at first, then faster, to imbibe.

There were only five or six of us still there when Leda slammed her glass down on the table. 'This is getting dull. I know.' She looked speculatively at the boys on either side of her. 'We'll play the truth game.'

'OK,' said Peanut, laughing.

I watched for Bill's reaction. He was slightly blurred by drink; he gave Leda a look and smiled. 'Haven't played that since I was fourteen.'

'About time, then,' Leda replied briskly.

We cleared a space for the bottle, and there was a moment of silence. Leda was enjoying herself. The bottle spun in the half-dark, skittered across the table, and came to rest pointing at Leda herself.

'All right, Leda, you start. What's the worst crime you've committed?' said Bill.

'Worst crime! Jesus. I dunno. Not sending my grand-mother a birthday card. Buying smack for my ex. Which is worse?'

The bottle spun again.

'Peanut,' Leda drawled. 'We'll start easy. What's your greatest desire?'

'To tell the truth,' he laughed.

Spin.

'Bill,' asked Peanut. 'When was the best sex you ever knew?'

'Er . . . dunno.'

'Come on!' she snapped.

'Well, all right – last night, with you, Leda,' Bill said, smirking.

'For God's sake! You're all liars, the lot of you.' She jumped up in a fury.

Later that night, when I stumbled to the kitchen for a glass of water, I glimpsed Bill and Leda at the end of the corridor. They were standing in each other's arms; their expressions were grave. She was speaking: by her tone, telling him something important. When I came back, I realised she was teaching him to waltz. Leda's head was inclined, revealing her long pale neck; sternly, she was intoning, 'One, two, three. One, two, three – now turn! – two three.' Every line of Bill's body expressed submission. If he had any secrets, he surely wasn't going to keep them for much longer.

Leda was at first given a room in Hostel No. 7, a miserable block at the other end of the city, but Edik Zelyony stepped in and, in a glimpse of his later success in business, instantly found an answer to two problems. Leda wanted to rent a room with a family; the Uvarovs wanted an *inostranka*, a foreign girl, as a lodger. When Mitya and I went to visit the following week, we found Leda smoking in the kitchen with Masha and Valya Uvarov. They already wore the look that, it seemed to me, expressed their relationship with Leda: admiring and a little uncertain, as though a beautiful, powerful, nervous bird had somehow flown into their apartment and a wrong movement might send it crashing towards freedom.

'You know, my family worried about me coming to Russia,' she said. 'But they had no idea . . . the scary place for me was New York. Did I tell you already about my boyfriend? He was older than me, you know, and I adored him, he was a photographer, so sexy. It was ages before I realised he was a junkie. I was so naïve, and he hid it from me, kind of protective in a way. Once I knew, he used to send me out to score, slap me around if there were problems getting hold of it. What a disaster.'

'At least it's over now.' Masha wanted to change the subject: it was the kind of thing she thought vulgar. She didn't like to associate it with their Leda. But we were interested.

'What did he look like?' asked Valya.

'Like a rock star, dark and skinny – I used to like that look. Not any more. Now I go for clean-cut men, athletic, you know, straightforward kind of guys.'

'You mean, like Bill?' I said.

Leda laughed. 'Bill! He's athletic, I agree. But I'm not sure he's so straightforward.'

'Do you know that for sure?'

'No. That's why I thought it would be interesting to play the truth game.'

'So you and he, are you –?'

'No! But he's keen. And I'm teaching him to waltz. I've never danced with a secret agent before. It's kind of exciting . . .'

Masha started laughing. 'But – *bozhe moi*, it's not possible!'

'What is it?'

'You said this boy is living with Peanut? Well, people say that Peanut's family is KGB, rather high-ranking – they have been for several generations.'

'No!'

We pondered this information.

'Who, do you think, follows whom? They take it in turns, perhaps?'

'Yes, who bugs whom?'

'It's absurd,' Valya said firmly. 'The stupidest nonsense I've ever heard. We're not living in the thirties, to be making such remarks about our friends. Peanut's family are in the army, just like Bill will be.'

We all agreed with her. It was nonsense.

'I'll tell you something, though,' said Mitya, after a few moments. 'I mean, this is progress, isn't it? Truly enlightened. Let them bother each other, and leave the rest of us in peace.'

Peanut had a tendency to disappear for a few days at a time. It was one of the things that made him *mutny*, cloudy, opaque. It's a common phenomenon, this cloudiness. The efforts required to achieve anything are so labyrinthine in Russia, the steps necessary to buy things 'on the left' or to obtain the right documents, that it becomes hard to live simply. Cloudiness starts to fog your days, your motives. People don't like to be questioned too closely. You guard your contacts and deflect inquiry. This time, however, the whole town was talking about his family.

There'd been a wedding last Saturday, his cousin, or perhaps his second cousin. The bride and groom had returned from ZAGS, the registry office. They'd been welcomed into the house with bread and salt, and the toasts and the feasting had begun. Soon the families had relaxed, no doubt they were leaning back in their chairs, mopping their faces, laughing and groaning as the mother of the bride carried in more meat, smoked fish, pressed everyone to try a little Jewish salad. That's how it is at Russian weddings, at least simple family occasions like this one. The father of the bride, like fathers of brides the world over, looks relieved, a little emotional, puts his arm around his wife and gives her a squeeze – 'We didn't do too badly, did we, after all?'

Sources disagreed over what happened next. Some said that two men forced their way into the room and grabbed the father of the bride. People the other side of the room didn't even realise it had happened. The two men clamped a hand over his mouth and dragged him out. In the shocked second before anyone reacted, they had thrown him down the stairwell. Others said that a fight broke out among the guests themselves, and that's how he ended up on the concrete three flights below. Whichever: by the end of the wedding, the man was dead.

As time went on and the police showed no sign of finding the killers, people drew conclusions. That was no coincidence, they said. Live by the sword, die by the sword. It was not as if this was an isolated incident. A secret war was being waged in those last few months of the Soviet Union that would shape the power blocs of the next decade, and Peanut's relation was just one of the casualties.

Something else was extinguished with him, too. We didn't miss it straightaway, yet, as the months of winter wore on, the sensation of loss grew stronger – a tiny thing, just a little flicker of optimism, a timid idealism that had been lit back in the summer when the mood was brave and fiery.

It was such a short time ago that people had tasted victory. At the end of August, when the coup orchestrated by KGB and Party chiefs had crumbled, furious crowds had surrounded the Central Committee building in Moscow. Dzherzhinsky's statue had been dragged from its pedestal outside the Lubyanka. 'Smash the KGB!' the placards had read. 'Send the Party to Chernobyl!'

In his book *Lenin's Tomb*, David Remnick described the scene inside the building. Party members and KGB officers were in a panic. How to destroy the evidence of their criminal activities over the past seventy years before the crowd surged in and lynched them all? They tried desperately to shred the most incriminating documents. But one by one the paper shredders juddered and broke: in their terror, the apparatchiks had forgotten to remove the paper clips. For a moment, the effects of their corruption must have appeared before them in horrifying clarity.

It didn't last. One of Yeltsin's first acts on taking power after the coup was to re-employ the majority of the Party functionaries and put the KGB back in business. Those who had not found more lucrative work in the private sector were back at their usual jobs the following Monday.

They had learnt their lesson, though. It was clearly no good relying on the state to provide for them. Now the collective nest was no more, they were forced to feather their own. In the next ten years, apparatchiks and secret police officers would gain control of all the major industries in the country. As directors of the new private companies that traded in Russia's vast resources of oil and gas, of diamonds, gold, wood and steel, they had access to wealth that they could only have dreamt of in the old days. Inevitably, there were disagreements between them and when these needed to be solved, perhaps an audience of wedding guests was welcomed. *Pour encourager les autres.*

Life in the hostel lurched on, as delightful as ever, although for me it had changed in one respect: I agreed with Mitya about the rumours. There were still hints that we were being supervised by some rather tolerant father figure. There were even moments when I felt anxious, as when I lost my wallet in town later in the winter. I was lucky, really – there was no money in it, nothing at all, in fact, except my student identity card, and a joint. For some days I felt the breath of the KGB on the back of my neck. But nothing happened. Perhaps it is still sitting in a file. Or perhaps the thief emptied the contents into a bin and sold the wallet, and the rest is paranoia – I don't know. The point was that the secret services were too busy to have much time for us that year. No doubt a little routine form-filling was going on; letters were read and people were called in for questioning now and again. Old habits die hard, particularly among bureaucrats. But the Cold War was over. Making money was the first priority now.

Leda realised this as well, it seemed. A month passed before I went round to the Uvarovs again, and when I did, Leda was there with her new boyfriend. Her flirtation with the secret services had come to nothing, although judging by appearances, there was no lack of interest on the part of the CIA. No, Leda was true to her word.

'Meet Sasha,' she drawled. 'He's a volleyball champion.'

Sasha smiled sweetly. He was sitting four-square in the corner, hands crossed tidily on his lap, and keeping quiet. He had clear brown eyes and shiny hair and a healthy sportsman's complexion. He certainly looked straightforward, although who, I thought, smiling back at him, could ever really tell?

Dmitri Donskoy and the Borders of Russia

You have your millions. We are numberless,
numberless, numberless. Try doing
battle with us!

Aleksandr Blok,
'The Scythians', 1918

Strange things had been happening on the train to Kiev. In class one day, our teacher Rita Yurievna told us about the visit she had just made to her relations. She was shocked.

'The police went straight through the carriage demanding money,' she said. 'Those Ukrainians! It's just pure greed, this nonsense about visas.'

'But, Rita Yurievna, the Ukraine has declared its independence.'

'How can they be independent? It's absurd! They're Russians, just like us. Kiev was the first capital of Russia. And what they call a language, well, it's more like a dialect. You know how they say, "Workers of the World, Unite" in Ukrainian? You used to see it on the banners: "Workers of the

World, Jump in a Heap!" In any case, in East Ukraine every-one's Russian, like my relatives.'

Rita Yurievna was not alone in holding these views. The Russians have long seen the Ukrainians as their jolly, dim-witted country cousins. Their accent, with its gutturals and rounded vowels, is the equivalent of Hardy's rustic burr and will reduce a roomful of the most liberal Russians to giggles. Khrushchev, who had the habit of wearing his embroidered Ukrainian shirt when he acted the buffoon for Stalin, embod-ied this image. Photographs of him banging his shoe on the podium at the United Nations and grinning toothily over a basketful of maize did nothing to raise the intellectual profile of his country.

Many Russians were faintly surprised, therefore, to find that the Ukraine had declared itself an independent state on 24 August (almost immediately the coup was resolved), not to say astonished when it became one of the largest countries in Europe. Governed from its ancient capital Kiev, it included the mining region of the Donbass, most of the Soviet navy and a huge number of nuclear missiles. On paper, the Ukraine had the capacity to become a major European power. And thus Voronezh suddenly found itself on an international border.

'It doesn't have the atmosphere of a border town,' Emily commented.

She was right; Voronezh had the sleepy, defenceless air of a city deep in the provinces.

'It's absurd!' Rita Yurievna repeated, frowning. 'Although,

of course, that was precisely how Voronezh began its life. The Battle of Kulikovo took place only a few kilometres north of here.'

We looked blank.

'You know the story of the Battle of Kulikovo?'

Our textbooks, open at the chapter concerning the declension of numerals in Russian – a tedious business – were quietly closed. Rita Yurievna was not often distracted, but we recognised this solemn look of hers. She began to describe the battle in the reverent, dramatic tone otherwise reserved for Pushkin. This was more than history: it was sacred myth.

In 1379, the Mongol khan Mamai vowed to crush the Russian princes utterly. It was almost a hundred and fifty years since the Golden Horde had bloodily subdued the Russians, but the Mongols had never ruled over them directly. Instead they exacted tribute from the Russian princes. In the late four-teenth century, however, Prince Dmitri of Moscow, later known as Donskoy, began to exert his authority over the other Russian princes and to resist paying up. It was this insubordination that enraged Mamai.

A whole year was spent mustering the Mongol troops. Half a million men gathered under Mamai's colours, included hired Armenians, Turks and a whole regiment of Genoese from Kaffa. On the other side of the Don, Dmitri's enemy Oleg of Ryazan waited to join the Mongols.

Mamai was jubilant. 'We are going to eat Russian bread

and grow rich on Russian treasure,' he crowed. 'The terror of me will crush Moscow.'

On 7 September 1380, Dmitri of Moscow's men crossed the river Don just north of Voronezh and ranged themselves on a wide, almost flat piece of ground bordered on each side by steep-banked rivers, known as Kulikovo field. That evening Bobrok of Volhynia took Prince Dmitri out onto the field and showed him how to judge his enemy's size by putting his ear to the ground. Dmitri listened and knew that the Russians were outnumbered by almost three to one. Bobrok and Vladimir the Brave were therefore ordered to lie back in the woods with their men and wait for the right moment to ambush the Mongols.

It was a bold plan. The Golden Horde was accustomed to fighting on the steppe where it could surround and engulf its enemies. For this reason, the Russians had chosen an enclosed space, where the Mongols' great number would be of only limited use. But Dmitri and his men were aware that Kulikovo could just as easily become a trap for the Russians. If the ambush worked, they had a chance, they agreed. But if it failed, their destruction was certain.

The morning of 8 September, the Virgin's Nativity, dawned misty; but by eleven o'clock the fog lifted and the shout went up: 'The Mongols are coming!'

The battle began. At two o'clock the Mongols almost broke through the centre of the Russian troops. By three the centre and the left wing were in confusion. It was a massacre: thousands, tens of thousands of Russians were killed. Bobrok and

Vladimir the Brave, hidden in the woods, received petitions from their men demanding to go to the assistance of their comrades. But Bobrok simply said, 'Wait a little longer.' By four o'clock Mamai was triumphant. Prince Dmitri's standard had fallen and Brenko of Bryansk was dead.

Only then did Bobrok and Vladimir lead their men onto the field. They struck the Mongols in the rear and flank with great fury, and the Mongols were filled with terror. They fled, pursued by Bobrok and his fresh troops throughout the night.

'It was a resounding victory for the Russians,' Rita Yurievna concluded. 'From then on they knew that the Mongols were not invincible.'

For centuries Russian folklore had described battles with their attackers from the east, enemies possessed of such terrible powers that even when sliced clean in half, they did not die but sprang back as two warriors. On Kulikovo field, however, Dmitri Donskoy recognised a truth known to every successful Russian ruler. To be victorious, they had to match and outdo their enemies' taste for blood; to be prepared to lose not only countless lives, but riches, peace and freedom to the fight. And this relentless sacrifice was demanded not only of soldiers on the front line, but of all Russians, who must be ready to give up everything for their country. It was necessary, simply in order to protect themselves. All Russia's expansionism, all its ruthless oppression of its own people sprang, it could be argued, from this basic desire: to establish borders of such impregnable strength that its people could at last feel secure.

Rita Yurievna led us briskly back to Russian grammar, and it was only at the end of the hour that she returned, obliquely, to the subject of the border.

'All one wants,' she said, 'is to sleep easy in one's bed. Isn't that right? And one's children to grow up peacefully. That's all. That's why we lived so well under Brezhnev. We were simply so relieved to be safe.'

· 9 ·

Free Day

I love the frosty breath,
and the confession of wintry steam.
Ah. I am I. Reality is reality.

Osip Mandelstam,
The Voronezh Notebooks, 1936

Mitya opened the steel door of his flat with a bottle of Soviet champagne in his hand. 'A drink in the morning and you're free all day!' he announced. 'Let's skip class.'

As I waited for the trolley bus ten minutes earlier, half frozen and the other half asleep, huddled in my elderly fake fur jacket and sneezing as each breath made the insides of my nostrils crackle, even then I had noticed a festive mood. The first sign was the station clock. I glanced at it, as always, to check that I wasn't early, and found it had stopped at twenty past four. No one could help me at the bus stop. Just a few months previously it would have been rare to find a wrist without a watch: now people were constantly asking each other the time. All the same, people brightened at the sight of the clock. 'Look at that!' they said proudly to each other. 'Frozen solid! How's that for a frost?'

I should have rung Mitya to check he was at home on his own: anything could happen in a freeze like this – school cancelled, offices closed. But the trolley bus wheezed towards the stop before I reached the telephone, and the combination of this holiday feeling, and the way trolley buses always reminded me of fat ladies, and a sudden bubble of joy made me run and jump on board. Mitya had a theory that extreme cold makes people optimistic, or perhaps that in the struggle for survival, optimism in the face of icy weather has proved most effective. He hadn't decided which way round it was but he pointed to penguins as an example. Penguins are clearly cheerful birds.

Now he stood in his hot, dark hallway, and beamed. 'It must be about minus twenty, I suppose,' he said, peeling layers of clothing from me. 'The perfect temperature – everything looks wonderful, it's too cold to work, the vodka's chilled by the time it's home from the kiosk . . .' He took my foot in his warm hands. 'Come on, drink the having-been-produced-for-export champagne,' he said. 'We've got nothing to lose but our chains.'

When we emerged, the champagne had propelled us into a perfect future. Snowdrifts had swaddled Voronezh a couple of days before; now the city glittered under a crust of ice. Light streamed from every surface.

We walked fast, in no particular direction. Outside the

Opera theatre a yardman was snapping a line of icicles with a hammer to prevent them from melting in the afternoon and falling on passers-by. The yardman swung his hammer and listened to the jangle as they hit the ground.

'Playing my xylo-thing,' he said, grinning.

'A yardman musician! Well, that's the Opera for you!' commented a lady in an astrakhan coat, who had also stopped to watch. 'There's nothing in the shops,' she added, cheerfully, 'so what can I do but stroll about?'

Lenin Square was criss-crossed with people walking arm in arm; as they came closer, emitting little puffs of steam, we saw they were wearing their best clothes, glossy fur coats and hats that smelt a little of mothballs – clothes that only came out when it was twenty degrees below. Rosy cheeks and noses peeped out from a fringe of Siberian fox. The two bars on Revolution Prospect were overspilling onto the pavement where men stamped and swung their arms, waiting for a little *vodochka* to warm them up. Children were tobogganing down the slope to the reservoir, now and again hitting lumps of ice and flying off into snowdrifts with yelps of joy. Those who did not have toboggans used trays or pieces of cardboard or just flung themselves onto their tummies like seals. Mitya and I found some board and shot down the slope, colliding with a sledgeful of children. I instantly fell off and landed in the same drift, a few metres below them, but they had already begun to climb again. They were so bundled up that their arms stuck out at right angles to their bodies. Their faces were purple with exertion, yet they could think of nothing but speeding down the hill again. They were bewitched.

> The boy, the little lord of his sleigh,
> the leader of the gang,
> rushes past, red as a torch.

I had just discovered Osip Mandelstam's *Voronezh Notebooks* and my thoughts were full of his ice-sharp images, and the sideways leaps between them.

In 1934, Mandelstam wrote his death sentence: a poem calling Stalin 'the Kremlin mountaineer/The murderer and peasant-slayer'. He was arrested and interrogated, and it seemed he would be sent from prison straight to the camps. But by a lucky twist, he and his wife were exiled instead, first to the north and then to Voronezh.

'The Voronezh of 1934 was a grim place, badly off for food,' Nadezhda Mandelstam, his wife, wrote in her autobiography. 'Dispossessed kulaks and peasants who had fled the collective farms begged in the streets. They stood by the bread stores and stretched out their hands. They had long since eaten their supplies of dry crusts brought with them in bags from their native villages.'

Collectivisation was starving the countryside, while the purges emptied the cities. The Mandelstams, as 'politically unreliable' citizens, were constantly harassed. Every aspect of their lives was a struggle: they had no money, nowhere to live. Mandelstam himself was sick and nervous, and prone to attacks of breathlessness if Nadezhda left him even for a day. And yet in the midst of this desperation, he wrote three long cycles of poems filled with wonder and love of life. The repressions that would kill him just three years later could not compete, it seems, with the spontaneous delight that the country aroused in him. The snow-clad expanses, the city lost in the limitless steppe like a boat at sea, the 'ten-figure forests' and the 'trains calling to each other in long-drawn-out whistles': these somehow, miraculously, gave him the freedom to write.

Most of this new work was composed on the move, as the poet walked through the back streets of Voronezh. He mumbled as he went, searching for the shape of a poem; finally, when he was satisfied, he would rush home and dictate it to Nadezhda. He was a well-known figure in the town, considered a bit soft in the head. The children ran after him and teased him – their nickname for him was 'the General', and I could imagine, watching these breathless, red-cheeked kids in the snow, what gales of giggles assailed their forebears when one of them dared to shout it out behind his back. 'Hey! General! Who're you talking to?'

Sixty-five years later, Mandelstam's words are no less immediate:

> I'll wonder at the world a little longer still,
> at the children and the snow.
> But a smile is like the road – it can't be faked,
> and is disobedient, not a slave.

At the hot-water pipes down by the reservoir, Mitya and I met Lapochka and Petya Pravda. We knew this place well, a cosy spot where one could sit and converse honestly and openly whatever the temperature. When we arrived, the boys were deep in discussion of a topic that has obsessed Russians throughout Soviet history: accommodation.

'Divided straight down the middle, you see,' Petya was saying as we approached. He shook hands with us. 'This is the renovation in my flat. I'm planning on making it into two parts, one for my mother and one for me, entirely separate.'

'But you'll barely be able to turn round.'

'Ah, but still – you haven't heard the brilliance of the plan yet. Entirely separate parts, yet linked at one vital point.'

'The kitchen?'

'Better than that. The fridge. I've designed a two-doored fridge with the motor down the side – she stocks it from that side, and I eat from this. Mother love at its most elemental.'

Lapochka got out a *papirosa* and began to tap the tobacco onto the ground. 'You'd have to talk to each other through the fridge, past the milk products. It'd be good. You'd never argue, would you? Hard to argue with a yoghurt?'

Petya passed a matchbox to Lapochka, who poured a little pile of marijuana out of it onto his palm. All that was left of the *papirosa* was an empty tube of cardboard and cigarette paper, which Lapochka began to pack with grass.

'Look,' said Mitya, 'look at the fishermen.'

From the hot-water pipes we gazed out onto the reservoir, now a snowy plain dotted with figures. They sat beside the

holes they'd sawed out for themselves, motionless, dark and
furry as otters. They neither talked nor gazed at the scenery.
They peered intently at their lines vanishing under the shadowy blue ice. It was clear that it was a matter of moments
before a monster, a prizewinner, leapt out at them.

As Lapochka twisted the end of the joint, Smokey turned
up with another friend. The Narcomen, as this lot were
known, had perfect timing in these matters. Petya Pravda
claimed he could smell it half a kilometre off, and classify it at
one hundred metres on quality, strength and entertainment
value. The last consideration outweighed the rest – he had a
horror of being bored. It was an oversensitivity caused by
the monstrous tedium of much of Soviet life. Queues, bureau-
cracy, the dreary verbosity of officialdom, the uniform
architecture – the Narcomen were in vigorous protest against
them all.

'When you are on the train to boredom, it's simple,'
explained Petya to me, speaking slowly in case the concept
was hard to follow. 'All you do is smash the window and jump
out to an unknown fate. Understand?'

It was not always easy to keep to this edict. Drink and
drugs helped, of course, but they were not the only ways to
jump off the train. Ideas were just as important to the
Narcomen – theatre design, philosophy, Latin American literature, performance art – anything new. Books and tapes
were passed from hand to hand, and suddenly the talk would
be all Borges, or Zoroaster, or Massive Attack. In this,
Voronezh had not changed since the eighties when, by the

process known as *magizdat*, cassettes of dissident music circulated the country, recorded and re-recorded until they were barely audible. Mitya had a tape that had been made in some flat in Moscow before perestroika. Through the crackle you could just make out the sounds of a party, people chatting, calling for more vodka, and then the hoarse, amused voice of a Russian punk, Petya Mamonov, singing: 'I eat rubbish, I drink from puddles, I'm a filthy . . . [here he achieved a tone of some menace] . . . pigeon. And yet . . . I can *fly.*' It could have been the Narcomen's anthem.

We smoked the joint and Petya began messing around; he took a run-up and launched himself onto an ice slide that some kids had made. He slid for twenty metres, knock-kneed and gangly, and landed with a crash.

The light enveloped everything; we were six dark spots on a landscape of blazing white reflection. Above us the glassy blue eye of the heavens was empty. I lay back and gazed into it, and after a minute or two the world flipped over and I was suspended above the sky, feeling the tug of its gravity deep in my solar plexus.

'Don't fall asleep, or you'll freeze,' said Mitya. 'Let's go.'

There was one more wonder awaiting me that day. We wandered along the edge of the reservoir to the other side of the bridge, where the beach was in summer; behind a grille lay a stack of pedaloes covered in snow. A solitary figure stood by the pedalo hut. As we came closer, I realised he was taking off his clothes. Hat, scarf, coat; then the jersey, shirt and vest came off to reveal a bony little chest. He was a slight man with a wispy beard; with a composed, sensible expression he was now slipping off his boots, two pairs of socks, trousers and baggy pink long johns. Each article was folded neatly and placed behind him.

Petya Pravda grinned at my horrified expression. 'He's a walrus,' he said, as if explaining.

'Yeah, and you're George Harrison! Are you sure it's not suicide?'

'No, no – watch,' they shushed me.

Now dressed only in black underpants, the walrus took a metal bucket in both hands. He raised it over his head and tipped it up, and we heard a strangled croak, as a small sea bird might emit at the sight of a polar bear's tonsils. Two gallons of icy water sluiced over the wretched man. But no sooner was it done than the walrus caught sight of us and, merrily towelling his back and his pitiful, blue-toned little belly, hallooed a welcome.

'Fine day, isn't it!' he shouted, whipping on his long johns, the trousers, boots, vest, jersey, coat and hat in a trice. His beard was frozen into crinkly panels and his face glowed a fiery red.

'One of the finest!' Lapochka called in reply.

The walrus stuffed his towel into a little rucksack and swung it over his shoulder, coming towards us with springy steps. 'Aaaaah, that feels good!' he announced. 'I never miss a day. Normally I go in the water, of course, but the hole froze so solid last night, I didn't have time . . . Until last year, my father and I always swam together, but now he's seventy, the doctors say he shouldn't. Fools!'

He saluted us and stomped off, and once he'd rounded the corner, the others looked at my expression and started laughing. For some reason, heaven knows why, it struck them as funny; Petya Pravda, in fact, was so overcome that he was forced to bend over and stamp his foot several times. It was as though we had achieved some snowy, bright, breathless peak; we were light-headed and triumphant, and there seemed to be no good reason for us ever to come down.

'Mityush,' I said when we arrived back at the hostel, 'we'll always be together, won't we?'

'Of course,' he answered. There was nothing more to say.

If I had to produce proof of a compassionate God, this would be one of my first exhibits: the blissful, lunatic assumption of the happy man that for him alone, time does not exist. Even Osip and Nadezhda Mandelstam felt it: just months before Osip was arrested for the second time, as they moved back to Moscow from Voronezh, Nadezhda wrote, 'Improbable as it may seem, we fell into an inexplicable state of calm and believed for some reason that our life was at last secure . . .'

Akhmatova, visiting them in Voronezh in 1936, saw their position more clearly:

> And the town stands locked in ice:
> A paperweight of trees, walls, snow.
> Gingerly I tread on glass;
> the painted sleighs skid in their tracks.
> Peter's statue in the square points to

crows and poplars, and a verdigris dome
washed clean, seeded with the sun's dust.
Here the earth still shakes from the old battle
where the Tartars were beaten to their knees.
Let the poplars raise their chalices
for a sky-shattering toast,
like thousands of wedding-guests drinking
in jubilation at a feast.
But in the room of the banished poet
Fear and the Muse stand watch by turn,
and the night falls,
without the hope of dawn.

· 10 ·

New Year, New Happiness

In general, our people are not too successful with
representative institutions.

Nikolai Gogol, *Dead Souls*, 1842

I met my father in St Petersburg for Christmas. The day I
arrived, I had the sensation that the city with all its monumental architecture was not as solid as it should be; the colours
were overluminous, the snowy street billowed beneath my feet
like canvas. When I arrived at my father's hotel, he hugged me
and looked at me intently. 'How are you feeling, Charlotte?' he
asked. 'You've got a fever, surely.' He was right, of course, and
I wasn't the only one: the whole country was in a fever, a fever
of finality. In a week's time, on New Year's Eve, the Soviet
Union would formally cease to exist.

It was a most elegant Christmas. We celebrated alone:
Orthodox Christmas falls on 7 January, and in any case New
Year is the important festival for Russians. My father and I
strolled along the canals and over the bridges, through the
fantastic labyrinth of the Hermitage and the idylls of Tsarskoe

Selo. We ate sparsely. On 25 December we sat on spindly gilt chairs at the Maly Theatre to watch *The Queen of Spades*, and in the interval a lady in a dark silk coat rushed up to my father and said in ringing English tones, 'Darling! How wonderful to see you here. I've got a box, there, I *always* come to St Petersburg for Christmas . . . Tomorrow I have a little salon, you must come.'

At dinner one night in a restaurant, we were placed next to the small dance floor. As we nibbled at caviar and smoked meats, a tall, serious girl danced before us in a long black dress, which she gravely removed. The little she was wearing underneath came off with no less dignity. I have never known anyone give off such an air of refined suffering when dancing naked. My father and I looked gloomily at the plates in front of us. It seemed impolite to tuck in, in the circumstances.

It was only when I had seen him off and boarded the train back to Voronezh that my temperature dropped and the world settled back into solidity. He'd left me with a suitcase full of good and useful things: a teapot, a huge bag of Smarties, and a Christmas cake wrapped in foil. It was 30 December, and even the conductress in my train carriage was feeling festive. She joked as she slotted our tickets into her leather ticket pouch.

'Going to spend the New Year with your family, eh? Quite right, use the railways while you can, it's only a matter of time before they're sold off to the capitalists!'

She laughed and the kindly, middle-aged couple occupying the bunks opposite joined in, demurring a little, 'Oh, come now –'

They were already in their royal-blue travelling tracksuits. Once the conductress had gone, the wife plumped down by the window, shifting her bottom until she had made a comfy hollow for herself. Then she nodded at her husband who pulled a bottle of champagne out of the sports bag under his feet.

'Well,' he said. 'Let's go then, shall we?'

The fourth member of our compartment, a pale, silent young man, managed a timid smile. 'Let's go!'

I had no bottle of my own to produce, but the Christmas cake went down well. The nice couple, who were engineers in the metal industry, helped themselves to second wedges and exclaimed at its tastiness. When we had been talking for a while, the pale young man joined in, volunteering the information that he was a violinist from Uzbekistan. His name, he told us shyly, was Genghis. Well, there was no stopping us after that. Mr Engineer reminisced about the walking holiday he had taken in Central Asia, oh, it must have been twenty years ago, before he'd met Mrs Engineer. She, meanwhile, was reminded of the Uzbek orchestra that she had heard in the Palace of Youth in Moscow once, how it had sent shivers up her spine.

'You're a very passionate people, I would say,' pronounced Mrs Engineer sagely. 'Of all the peoples of the Soviet Union, I'd think – of course I don't know for certain – but I'd *think* that the Uzbeks were the most passionate.'

'Yes, you're right,' nodded Mr Engineer. 'Full of passion. I noticed it on my tour.'

Genghis blushed.

'Not that there is any more Soviet Union,' sighed Mrs Engineer. 'No more friendship of peoples.'

'Yes there is, dear,' said her husband. 'Look at us all together. And the champagne's not finished!'

She rolled her eyes. 'Always the optimist,' she said, and the moment of anxiety passed. I passed around the cake again and Mrs Engineer described to me her recipe for the apple pie called a charlotka, until our glasses were empty and it was time for bed.

Perhaps it was the fever, or perhaps it was the champagne; in any case, in the morning I overslept, and was woken by Mrs Engineer as we rumbled over the iron bridge across the Voronezh river. She had changed out of her tracksuit into a red-and-black check dress that made it difficult to focus. My eyes slid shut again with the effort . . . Suddenly we were in the station and the conductress was roaring at me. 'Get up, get up, what kind of a way is this to behave on the railways!'

I scrambled off the train, still half dozing, and it was only as I was almost at the hostel that a rush of adrenalin jolted me awake. My passport, money, contact lenses and all the presents I had bought for New Year – they were in a bag tucked safely under the bunk, and now, no doubt, on the way to the Ukraine.

The platform was empty by the time I returned. There was only one guard leaning on his snow shovel and gossiping with a friend.

'Where's the train from Moscow?'

'Gone, *dyevushka*. Finished.'

'But where is it now? I left something on it –'

'Oh, it's being cleaned.' The guard looked at my expression and heaved a sigh. 'Walk down the tracks, that way, and you'll find it, if you really have to.'

'You say – walk down the tracks?'

'That's right – just keep going. Watch out for trains, that's all.'

It was a muffled, snowy morning and the crunch of my footsteps was loud. At the end of the platform I found a flight of steps down to the tracks, which stretched out ahead until they blurred and vanished, bordered by firs thick with snow. The spacing of the sleepers was just slightly longer than my normal pace. Everything was quiet.

After some minutes I came upon a young man digging at the side of the tracks.

'Excuse me,' I hailed him. 'I'm looking for Train Number 9, from Moscow –'

'Oh yes,' he nodded, as if he'd known what I was going to ask. 'Keep walking until you reach the *budka*, and ask again. Ask at the *budka*,' he repeated, and turned back to his task.

I didn't know what a *budka* was, but he was no longer listening. So I continued along the tracks. A long time passed, and then I saw an old man making his way slowly towards me.

'Please, I'm looking for Train Number 9 –'

He looked me up and down and shook his head. 'No, daughter,' he said. '*Dalshe*. You must go further.'

Again I continued along the tracks. It was hard work striding from sleeper to sleeper, and my feet were frozen inside their boots. At last I made out a structure in the distance, a tall, narrow hut with stairs leading up to the first floor. There seemed to be a light in the window. At the top of the stairs, the door was standing slightly open. I looked inside and a pair of figures like large plums in railway uniform swivelled to look at me in astonishment.

'Forgive me for disturbing you, but I'm looking for the *budka* – well, in fact, my bag – it's being cleaned, the train – from Moscow –'

'Moscow?' said one, doubtfully.

'Your bag?' said the other. They began to quiver.

'Yes, on the train from Moscow, it's being cleaned in a siding –'

They could hold back no longer. Guffaws burst from them. 'How did you find us?' they finally managed to ask. 'Where are you from?'

'Well, England.'

'England!' They jumped up and made me take one of their seats, having first wiped it with a sleeve. 'Train Number 9, eh – don't worry, we'll find it for you. We'll give Sergei a shout, over there –' and they began to make calls on a huge oily telephone, still chuckling and muttering to each other, 'An *anglichanka*! In our *budka*!'

So this was a *budka*. I looked about me. It was built of riveted metal plates. On two walls, there were large, rectangular windows arranged in 'portrait' rather than 'landscape' fashion, running from roof to floor. I suddenly realised what it was: half a train carriage, standing on one end.

Outside the *budka*, a huge red locomotive hissed to a halt. The plums hopped nimbly onto a running board beside the driver.

'Hup!' they called out, swinging me aboard, and we chugged away down the snowy line.

'The bag's got her passport in – English,' they told Sergei.

'Don't want to lose that,' said Sergei, putting his foot down. After a few minutes we came to the siding. 'There she is,' he called out over the noise of the engine. 'What carriage were you in?'

Train Number 9 showed no sign of activity. The windows were dark, there was no movement inside. My passport was surely fetching a nice price at the back of the railway station, with a slice of Christmas cake thrown in. At carriage 12, I climbed down into the snow. It was deeper here, and I had to force my way through to the door. Sergei and the plums were peering out of the engine window. I knocked, feeling ridiculous.

Almost instantly, the door swung open and a willowy man in overalls made an elaborate bow.

'Charlotta Hobson, I suppose?' he said, and handed me my bag.

We dropped the plums back at their *budka*, leaving the cake with them, and Sergei took me on to the station. We rattled over those rails and blasted on the horn like devils. A glimmer of sun was showing on the edges of the fir trees, and Sergei took a couple of swigs from a filthy bottle of spirit. It was almost ten o'clock on the last day in the history of the Soviet Union.

Back in the hostel, I pushed open the door and found the room had turned silver. Ira had pinned hundreds of single strands of tinsel to the ceiling. You couldn't see much, but it brushed your face pleasantly as you moved through it. I could just make out Joe smoking, Ira chopping onions into a frying pan, and Emily, head down, searching for something in the bags under her bed. The TV was on with the volume turned down and the Waterboys were booming out of the stereo.

'*Privyet*,' said Ira, grinning. 'How's things?'

'Hey!' said Emily, pulling her head out from under her bed. 'You're back! What did you bring us?'

The atmosphere in the hostel was strained and excitable. In previous years most of the students would have gone home for the New Year holidays, but with the inflation many couldn't afford it, and the place was full. In the kitchen, people were struggling to cook for tonight's feast. The cleaners had gone on strike ten days previously, the heap of rubbish in the corner reached five foot up the walls, and still people were adding more. Occasionally it settled and slid further out into the room, and everyone who was fighting and shouting over the few hobs that worked would curse and kick it out of the way.

Now and again, someone would say, 'Hey, everybody, let's remember that it's a holiday today. Let's wish each other peace and good spirits.'

And someone else would growl, 'Yeah right, peace to you, you idiot. When are you going to cork your ears up, the air blowing through your head's disturbing me.'

The Armenians had already begun their celebrations, and Garo was lurching along the corridor, trying to hug the *Komendant*. A tiny girl in a pinafore saw them coming and hid in the stairwell, clasping the bowl of coleslaw she'd been making to her chest. But they were heading for the stairs and they soon spotted her.

'It's Thumbelina!' they cried. 'Come here, my beauty, come and celebrate with us. Look what a tasty little salad she's made, the little mousekin!' and on and on. She blushed furiously, dodged under their arms and hurried away to her room, muttering under her breath.

Emily and I went downstairs to Room 99. An invitation had been awaiting my return, decorated with a picture of Santa Claus holding a samovar. 'The Great Chamber of 99 requests the pleasure of your company in greeting 1992,' it announced. 'Celebrations will commence with a Grand Parade in formal dress.' And beneath, in capitals: 'THIS UNIQUE EVENT WILL NEVER BE REPEATED.'

There were to be fifteen of us, and Liza Minelli was cooking a sort of goulash with paprika. She kept coming in and out, searching for more ingredients and telling us how delicious it was. 'You won't believe it!' she repeated each time.

'It'll blow you to fragments!' Emily and I sat down with Nina to peel a bucket of potatoes.

At four o'clock, Viktor came in, announcing, 'Happy New Year.' He poured all of us a few grammes.

'Isn't it a bit early?'

'In Vladivostok,' he explained.

As the sky darkened, the new year swept towards us across the endless steppe.

This unique event was indeed unlikely to be repeated. From midnight, we would be living in a new country, the Russian Federation, a country with a new flag, a new anthem and a new constitution. The command economy would be abolished, and free-market economics would transform the way Russians lived and worked. The legal code would have to be rewritten, along with the marriage service, the history books and the maps. New banknotes would have to be printed; Soviet slogans all over the country would be taken down; institutions, streets, whole cities would change their names. The army, much depleted, would have to be brought home within the country's new borders with the independent states of Latvia, Lithuania, Estonia, Belarus, Ukraine, Georgia, Azerbaijan, Uzbekistan, Tajikistan. For the second time in the twentieth century, Russia was starting afresh.

Which, as Mitya pointed out at dinner that evening, gave us more than enough toasts to last until it was all over. We were sitting on the beds in Room 99, crammed around a long table that the girls had somehow assembled. Plate after plate of *zakuski*, snacks to be eaten with the vodka, lay before us; when the plates ran out, they'd turned to saucepan lids and pieces of paper.

'*Bozhe moi*, Mitya, you're not going to torment us with politics all evening, are you?' cried Liza Minelli. 'Eat, everyone, drink. It's a party.'

We fell upon the food, and Viktor, who was there with a new girlfriend barely more than a schoolgirl, made a small speech about the fact that vodka was pure spirit, or near enough, and therefore should not be tainted by worldly things such as politics or money ('meaning you should always drink other people's,' interjected Tanya). Vodka, he continued, should only come into contact with the finer things in life: poetry, and love – and so he proposed a first toast for the evening, which was, 'To the hymen.'

The goulash arrived and worked its magic: as the first taste hit the roof of the mouth, a fierce little fireball flew up both nostrils and exploded behind the eyes. A chorus of snorts stopped all talk and Liza Minelli looked pleased with herself. 'I warned you,' she said complacently. 'I said it would blow you to fragments.'

Yakov was describing previous New Years, spent with his parents. They, like millions of others, never missed the yearly showing of the film *The Irony of Fate, or Enjoy your Steam Bath* – a romantic comedy based on the premise that in every town in the Soviet Union there is an identical street called Builders' Street, lined with blocks of flats each furnished with the same furniture, with the same pictures on the walls and books on the shelves. Just as comic was the New Year report from the bourgeois capitalist states: 'In Spain,' the commentator would pronounce in funereal tones, 'they will not be greeting the New Year joyfully. Unemployment runs at so many per cent, so many thousands have no home . . . In Washington, it won't be a happy New Year either. Sixty per cent of the country's wealth is concentrated in the hands of five per cent of exploitative capitalists . . . As for Paris –' and so on. The same footage of homeless children would appear year after year, until they became fond of it. 'There's the one with a wart again,' they'd say. 'Still no older.'

This year, however, we turned on the TV at midnight and watched the huge red hammer-and-sickle flag on the Kremlin being lowered against the dark sky. There was a moment's pause, and then the Russian tricolour was slowly raised in its place.

It should have been a great moment, the lowering of the tyrants' sign – and yet the red flag with its hammer and sickle looked so brave and bold in comparison with these dreary red, white and blue stripes. We cheered, and then a pang of nostalgia silenced everyone. The imagery of their childhood was being laid aside and the socialist ideals that had been taught along with it were now obsolete. For children of the Brezhnev years, the real and the ideal were plainly delineated; no one felt any sadness at the end of Party hegemony. The ideals, though, were different. It was as though the government had suddenly announced that love did not conquer all.

Yuri jumped up and started banging a saucepan lid. 'Forward, comrades! Let's sing our anthem for the last time!'

We agreed noisily and set off down the corridor, banging saucepans and cups, and bellowing the Soviet hymn.

> 'Indestructible Union of free republics,
> Joined together for all time by great Russia!
> All hail the one, powerful Soviet Union,
> Created by the will of the people!'

'Farewell to our flag!' shouted Oleg.

'Hurrah!' cried the crowd. People were coming out of their rooms and joining in. One of the English boys produced a hammer-and-sickle flag and ran in front, waving it and banging on doors. A swelling of voices continued with the chorus:

> 'Glory to our free Fatherland
> The friendship of peoples is our safe stronghold!
> The Party of Lenin, the power of the people
> Will lead us to the triumph of Communism!'

'Farewell to the Party of Lenin!' yelled someone.

'Hurrah!'

'Farewell to our Young Pioneer uniforms with their little caps!'

'Hurrah!'

'Farewell to "Workers of the World Unite!"'

'Hurrah!'

'Farewell to the Communist Party!'
'Hurrah!'
'Farewell to Lenin! Let him point somewhere else!'
'Hurrah!'
'Farewell! Farewell! Farewell!'

Much later that morning, about six, when Mitya had gone home and Jim and I were just finishing up the champagne, Viktor appeared and said, 'Let's go out, see what's on the streets.'

'Oh, Viktor, I'm finished, I'm just going to bed,' I tried.

'Come on! It's the first day of a new era, don't you want to congratulate people?'

So Jim, Viktor and I set off. It was cloudy and warm outside, and the streets were almost empty. Viktor marched about making gestures like a poet. An elderly couple were walking their elderly dog. 'Happy New Year!' Viktor announced in his stentorian voice and they smiled, a little taken aback. Jim found Pioneer badges for sale in a kiosk; they bore a flame surrounded by the motto 'Always ready!' We pinned them to our hats. Viktor was striding towards a tram. 'Happy New Year,' he greeted the driver, blowing her a kiss.

We were heading, inexorably, for the station, partly because I had a vague idea that we might see Sergei or the plums again, partly because we were always attracted to the railways, the trains idling on the way to Sofia, Odessa and the Far East. There was always commotion and bustle there, even at six o'clock on New Year's Day. The waiting room was filled with refugees from the wars in the Caucasus who shifted and moaned on their bundles. People hurried to and from trains, policemen strolled about proprietorially, and the eternal line of babushkas gossiped by their buckets of meat pies, boiled potatoes and bottles of Moskovskaya vodka with crooked labels. Viktor walked among them, congratulating them, and where he went I followed with the packet of Smarties my father had left me, doling them out into mittened palms. 'Little chocolates,' I explained. 'For health and success.'

The long-distance trains were standing close by and as we wandered along, we saw that one of the windows was open. Without any further discussion we scurried across the tracks, climbed in and settled down to sleep and wake up the devil knows where. We'd only been there a couple of minutes before the conductress came upon us blazing with fury.

'Happy New Year,' said Viktor gently, kissing her inflamed cheeks.

She suddenly simpered and looked at the floor, saying, 'Oh well, and new happiness to you all too.'

So we went to Lipetsk, Viktor's home town, instead. The early-morning passengers on the *elektrichka* wore stoical expressions as they huddled in the corners away from the broken windowpanes. They watched with a certain pleasure as Viktor and Jim took their shirts off and we sang for the two hours of the journey, a sort of *Schadenfreude* for us ruining our health sitting in draughts like that. We took our revenge by inciting their husbands to drink with us.

'Sasha, come on. Join us!'

Sasha's wife muttered furiously in his ear and he raised a limp hand in our direction to say, 'Thanks, guys, but I really can't, you understand the situation.'

But we showed no mercy and kept on at him. 'Join us! It's a holiday. Only one, really!'

Two days we spent in Lipetsk, and I remember little of it but a wall entirely covered by a huge reproduction of a lake surrounded by birch trees, and dancing with a crowd of blonde girls and dark husbands, and more vodka, and the feel of a brown blanket under my cheek as at last I slept some time that evening. No other coherent thought crossed my mind.

But when we arrived back in Voronezh, Mitya was waiting, furious. Why hadn't I told him where I was going? Why hadn't I rung? He'd worried. He'd felt a fool, not knowing.

To me, with my hangover, it seemed only reasonable that such a new year should take longer than usual to be born. But Mitya was hurt. At the end of our first serious argument, he walked away from me, sticking his hands in his pockets and hunching his shoulders. I should have gone after him. Instead I stood on the hostel doorstep and watched until he disappeared.

11

The House of the Deaf and Dumb

A newspaper cartoon shows a lone demonstrator waving
a banner that reads 'I don't understand anything'.

The Times, 25 October 1991

Lapochka swung open the door to his room before we had
time to knock.

'Look at the doorbell,' he boasted.

A light bulb flashed when the button was pressed.

'It's a house for the deaf-and-dumb!' He grinned at Mitya
and me, delighted. 'It's full of surprises. I had an idea the
house would be very silent, but in fact they make so much
noise. They are always slamming doors, crashing pots in the
kitchen, stomping up and down the corridor – and I can
hardly ask them to be quiet, can I. Would you like tea?'
Lapochka arranged some chairs around his table. He had
been given the job of boiler-stoker for the winter in the house,
in return for which he received a pitiful salary and this room
full of old stage sets and half-finished canvases. 'The previous
boiler-stoker was an artist,' he explained. 'Anyway – I've only

learnt one concept in their language, and that's this,' he tapped his forehead. 'Guess what it means.'

'Crazy? Clever?'

'Thinking? Understanding? Got a headache?'

'No, no, no. Think laterally. It means grass! Two old guys here sell it to me. The first time they came to my door and stood there tapping their heads, well, I was a little bemused. Up till then, our communication had mainly consisted of the scenario where they'd stamp their feet and go "brrr", and I'd stoke up the boiler a bit. But the head-tapping confused me until they brought out the grass. Then I started laughing, and they laughed too, and now we've got a deal going.'

There were a great number of deaf-and-dumb people. At the beginning their quietness made them difficult for me to see: when everything was unfamiliar, the noisy claimed my attention first. Later the pool of silence around them rang louder than voices, and I found myself noticing the deaf-and-dumb everywhere. In the shop known as the Iron, or down at the station, they would be standing in a group, having an animated, silent conversation. At the war memorial and other sights, they were usually pointing excitedly. There were particular bars where they met, silently, to get rollicking drunk. I saw them parting at bus stops with a slap on the back and the signal that we would use to mean 'telephone me'. This was one of their many mysteries that I never managed to penetrate.

Lack of hearing aids and speech therapy, or rubella, or radiation – who knows why there were so many? They kept themselves separate, and even Lapochka did not really manage to make friends with them. When he tried to ask the old guys on his corridor about their lives, they grinned and gave each other a look. Then one covered his mouth, and the other his ears. Lapochka understood. 'Hear no evil, speak no evil.'

In the Soviet Union, of course, invisibility had been their lot. The mad, the handicapped, the homeless and the poor were not suitable participants in the Soviet experiment. How was the perfect society to be formed using imperfect materials? they reasoned, without quite expressing it so bluntly. What's more, how could citizens have faith in the society they were building if they were surrounded by half-wits and cripples? Just as we sweep the streets clean of litter for sanitary reasons, so we must ensure that our cities are free of these unfortunate elements.

The segregation began at birth: Ninety-five per cent of physically or mentally handicapped babies were removed from their families. Soviet medicine recognised a condition called 'oligophrenia' (literally: having a small brain). Children diagnosed as oligophrenics were further classified as 'imbecile', 'idiot' or 'feeble' and brought up in institutions run by the Ministry of Social Protection, where the exhausted and ill-trained staff did little more than feed them. The conditions were bad, perhaps most of all for those 'oligophrenic' children who, it turned out, had purely physical disabilities – who had been removed from their family, surrounded by emotionally and mentally disturbed children, left to fend for themselves and to grow without stimulation or attention of any kind.

People who developed mental illnesses later in life were spirited away to various destinations. Some were put in institutions; many others ended up in and out of prison for antisocial behaviour. Others became part of the underground world that inhabited the edges of Soviet life and was rather haphazardly concealed from the rest of society. Before the Olympics in 1980, for example, the tramps and alcoholics were simply picked up from the streets of Moscow and dumped a hundred kilometres from the centre of town. By the time they got back to the centre, with any luck, all the foreigners would have left.

Lately, however, the streets had begun to change. The underclass was coming out of hiding. An old man in an astrakhan coat and ancient felt boots buttonholed me on Revolution Prospect one day, saying, 'You don't want to wear trousers, *dyevushka*. That way the devil gets in, understand?'

'But what am I to wear, then?'

'In Central Asia they wear chiffon. Chiffon chuffon. Understand?'

He was one of those, like Johnson, who had somehow kept on travelling all over the Soviet Union in the days when others needed a permit for a shopping trip to Moscow. Johnson came up to Mitya and me one afternoon in Koltsov Square, asking for a cigarette, and when we offered him a bottle of beer, he sat down with us and told us something of his life. Tattoos curled and interlocked over his face and wrinkled, bald head. He had been homeless, a *bomzh*, for twenty years and more. Summers he spent in the Crimea, where travellers from all over the Union lived in caves and revelled through the hot nights. He'd been in the Far East and in Leningrad, and he'd lived some years in Central Asia about which he said only that the Asians were good people, but they ate nothing but rice, which was why they were so small. For that reason, they'd never rule like the Russians.

The worst times, he told us, were in prison. Johnson rolled back his sleeves and showed us his ageing biceps, decorated with chains, guns and a swastika. If either Mitya or I had had any experience of prison, we could have read them like a diary. Some showed what his crime was, where he'd served time and how long. Others revealed his rank in the prison hierarchy and so how much respect he deserved. Johnson particularly pointed out the swastika; it showed he was one of the tough guys. The weakest, he told us, were given tattoos by force. Tattooed teardrops on a man's cheeks meant that anyone was free to force him into any service. Those men rarely survived.

When Johnson was free, he would stay in a place for a few months, even a year, and then his head would start to torment him. The voices would marshal at his back and, almost without noticing, he'd pull on his boots and walk out into the great singing steppe where there was no shelter and not a crust of bread awaiting him. He was wizened and jittery from all his adventures but, he explained, he couldn't stop himself.

'Those voices chase me out,' he said. 'Lord knows why.'

Beggars of all kinds were appearing in the centre of town. There were Russians: old women who sat flat on the icy pavement and gaunt men who knelt, faces turned to the ground, and held up cards that read, 'God have mercy on me, I'm hungry.' Such a thing had not been seen since the famine after the Great Patriotic War. There were Caucasian refugees carrying their babies and repeating the story of their flight from the south; most people brushed past them suspiciously: everyone knew how rich and wily they were, those Caucasians – they passed those babies from hand to hand, poor little mites, to get more money out of the soft-hearted. It was hard to see how they spent all their riches. They were largely Armenians, living in the railway station and wearing cloth shoes that they'd patched in several places. Grief had worn them almost transparent.

There were also gypsies. I saw a group of gypsy women burst upon the outdoor market one grey afternoon, shouting to each other and moving quickly among the crowd. They wore layers of raucous scarves and frills, orange petticoats and pink–red shawls tied around their waists. Gold and sequins flashed from their arms as they elbowed shoppers out of their way. They offered their goods to sell with threats and laughed hoarsely when they were refused. Cursing them, the crowd turned their backs until the gypsies were gone. All the Russians despised and feared the gypsies. They'd steal the bread out of your mouth and give you the evil eye after-wards. They were not governed by the same laws as normal people; they were the harbingers of chaos. Two gypsies jumped on my trolley bus one day: 'Pregnant woman,' the man shouted, forcing a way for him and his companion towards the seats. 'Pregnant woman!' Two old men stood up meekly, while the man and his companion, a blade-thin girl of perhaps sixteen with a jingle of jewellery and kohl-rimmed eyes, took their seats and laughed in their faces. Opposite, a pale, solemn baby in his mother's arms stared at them and burst into furious tears when she tried to turn his face away. I would have gone with the gypsies, if they'd wanted to kidnap me.

I asked them once, on a whim, if I could stay the night with them. They were camped on a piece of waste land out towards the road to Moscow. Mitya and Edik were buying cigarettes. The woman that I asked laughed, and said, 'Better let me tell your fortune.'

'Let me just sit here and chat, then. We'll drink tea together.'

She looked dubious. 'I'll have to ask my baron,' she answered at last. 'Wait over there, and I'll find him.'

I joined Mitya, Edik and the others, who looked at me with disgust. 'They're dirty, Charlotte, what do you want with them?'

'Aren't you afraid of diphtheria? And tuberculosis?'

At last a squat man in stonewashed jeans approached us. 'You want to talk to the baron,' he stated flatly. 'He's away . . . he won't be here today.'

'Come on, we have to go,' Edik broke in. 'What's interesting about them?' he said, as we got back in the taxi. 'They're dangerous.'

And to most Russians, they were. Not just because of their thievery and their diseases, but because of the breath of anarchy that they released onto the streets. Like devils, they were, come to tempt us.

Anarchy was not new to Voronezh. As a border town, it had been barely controlled by Moscow until the end of the eighteenth century, inhabited by escaped serfs, schismatics fleeing persecution, and smugglers. The Cossacks who bred their famous horses in the region acknowledged no authority but their own. As late as 1765, when the Bishop of Voronezh visited a village in his diocese, he encountered a procession bearing a beribboned young man – a representation of Yarylo, the god of fertility. It was, a contemporary lamented, 'a half-pagan, half-barbarian region'.

Even in the 1930s, during the purges, Mandelstam detected an underlying spirit of dissent which he considered to be 'the free spirit of the borderlands'. In one village he found the members of a sect – the jumpers – who were persecuted in Tsarist times. There was chaos in the village because a short time before his visit the jumpers, speaking in tongues, had announced the date on which they would with one holy leap reach Paradise. Nadezhda Mandelstam described the scene: 'The sectarians had fixed a day on which they would take off for heaven, and, convinced that by next morning they would no longer be of this world, they gave away all their property to their earthbound neighbours. Coming to their senses when they fell to the ground, they rushed to recover their belongings, and a terrible fight broke out.'

In another village, the Mandelstams found the villagers were the descendants of exiles and convicts of the eighteenth century. Although the streets were now called after Soviet heroes, the villagers proudly repeated the old street names which commemorated their forefathers' activities: Strangler's Lane, Embezzler's Lane, Counterfeiter's Row.

This part of Voronezh's history, however, was little known or appreciated by the 1990s. For many people, the rabble that had begun to appear on the streets since perestroika was proof that the so-called democratic system was dragging their country into shame and disorder. Their town suddenly seemed strange to them, and dangerous. It was then that the hissed warnings began: don't go on the bus at night, don't walk at night, don't go to the market on your own, don't talk to Caucasians. These people – good, responsible citizens all of them – even regretted the end of the *propiska*, the residence permit, which had more or less prevented free movement within the Soviet Union. They were the ones who would tell you that Russians could only be ruled by the rod: look at our history! We're an Asiatic people, we're not European, they would explain. Russia is a great country – we just need a strong leader to bring us order.

They were right, of course, that this explosion on the streets meant misery to many. Old people suffered the most. The housing shortage made them vulnerable to New

Russian property developers, who tricked them out of their apartments. An old woman appeared in the stairwell of a friend's apartment one winter day – he saw her standing by the radiator as he left for work, waiting for someone, perhaps. In fact she was homeless and sick. Later that day she went up to the top floor, lay down on the cold steps, and died. There were many like her.

And yet for other members of the underclass it was a time of liberation. Johnson the *bomzh* told Mitya and me, 'A whole year's gone by without prison.' He couldn't tell us why, but he added wistfully, 'I'm going to the Novosibirsk region. They say it's beautiful there, with forests and lakes . . .'

His tone reminded me of the dreams of the Russian peasantry in the nineteenth century, of a utopia on the White Waters of the Altai mountains. Inspired by some omen, whole villages would suddenly set out towards these mythical lands, leaving their houses and fields behind. In 1856, not realising that the Crimean War had already ended, thousands of serfs departed on foot for the Crimea in the belief that the Tsar would set free all those who fought in the campaign.

And indeed, similar stories began to circulate in Voronezh in 1991. The Americans were about to open a factory in Voronezh, and all those who worked there would be given visas to the USA. The government was going to announce an immediate redistribution of land. And it was funding investigations into alien landings in the Voronezh region, as there had been so many sightings: one had even been reported by the TASS news agency – humanoid giants, three or four metres high with very small heads, had landed in a vehicle like a shining ball right in the centre of the city – Koltsov Square, or thereabouts.

Why not? Stranger things were happening all around. It was clear, now, that the grey materialism of the Communist regime was too tight to contain all of life. Chaos, passion and the old superstitious Russian magic had burst the seams, and now reality was layered and raucous.

So I was hardly surprised when the Horse told me about the deaf-and-dumb people. It was late one night at the bar in the Theatre of the Young Spectator. We were talking about Lapochka's housemates when the Horse sloped towards me and swore me to secrecy.

'You mustn't ever let them see you know,' he whispered. 'But they can hear, really, and speak.'

'What?'

'The deaf-and-dumb people. In reality they aren't. I drank with them one day, you see. We all went out to the vodka bar on Koltsov Square. That's where they all go, they call it the White Horse . . . And I bought them drinks and they bought me drinks and I think they must have put something in them, too, because I started feeling very hazy and you know that's not like me . . . everything was looking unsteady . . . and then one of them suddenly said, You know I can talk if I want. But I don't want . . . And another one said, We're underground, three kilometres underground . . . I remember particularly, three kilometres.'

'Then why do they pretend?'

'They have their reasons,' said the Horse, shrugging. 'Who knows why?'

He grinned his toothy grin and changed the subject. The Horse liked a mystery.

12

Little Pavlik

Is there room here, perhaps, to tell the story of little Pavlik? Whose diminutive size was the source of so much amusement. 'Little Pavlik!' people would call, pretending to search for him. 'Have you slipped down behind your bed? Been crushed under your blanket? You've not been trying to shave again, have you? How many times have we told you, that's for big boys, not little Pavlik.' They'd laugh and Pavlik would summon a smile, although who knows, it may have been then that the proper use of a razor first occurred to him.

Pavlik was, I think, eighteen. He must have been about four foot eleven, very slight and pale, with soft, colourless hair and a large forehead that sloped into a weak chin. His eyes flickered away from direct contact, but his mouth had an aggressive cast that only increased his comic potential. Just occasionally, when he thought himself unobserved, his large head drooped and revealed the nape of his neck. There was something horrifying about its slenderness.

His size, you see, was not hereditary. Pavlik had grown up in a children's home, fed on porridge and scraps of oily fish. All the inmates of Soviet institutions were badly fed, from the pride of the Red Army to the prison camps, but the orphans, of course, never recover from the effects of malnutrition and early misery. His parents had died, and his grandmother, old and weak herself, couldn't take on the burden of a young child. She had only her pension to live on – how would she feed a growing boy? He'd be better looked after by the state which cared for each of its children like a father and a mother. She left him at the children's home with a small bag of clothes and a knitted puppy, promising that if he worked hard, she would fetch him soon. Pavlik waited, listening out for her voice in his sleep. Years passed, the puppy unravelled under its burden of love. When nothing remained but a soggy woollen ear, Pavlik was called into the director's office and told that his grandmother had died some time before.

'We decided to wait until you were older before telling you,' said the director. 'It's our policy.'

Pavlik worked hard, just as his grandmother had told him. It was exceptional for a child from a home to get a place at university, but Pavlik was in his second year already. He was an intelligent boy, he would work in an office one day, have a suit, an apartment. But for the time being he lived in the hostel, and moved along its greenish corridors with a familiarity that made me sad. He never complained about the showers, like we did, or the claustrophobia. In the afternoons he lay on his bed, which was unusually comfortable by hostel standards. I exclaimed at it once and Pavlik's face lit up.

'It's a good bed,' he told me, seriously. He had two mattresses, and another standing against the wall to form a sofa back. He patted them with pride. 'These are my own, you see. I bought them.'

They were his refuge, his own mattresses. Sometimes he would stay there until the evening, sleeping and eating pieces of bread. He was little enough to stretch out in the institutional iron bed frame, which gave the rest of us cramp and froze our toes. His possessions packed neatly into his locker. Little Pavlik, too short to kiss girls or to be popular. Brought up on Soviet rations, it was as though he had turned out regulation Soviet size, to fit the low-ceilinged rooms and the shoddy furniture without protesting. Why protest? Didn't the state do the best it could for its orphans?

During the course of that winter, however, something gave way in Pavlik. The teasing didn't help. A rumour got around that at least one part of Pavlik had not been stunted by bad nutrition. The boys exclaimed about it when they came back from the showers, joked and widened their eyes. Somehow it gave them *carte blanche* with Pavlik, now that he could be envied.

'Come and have a little drink, little one,' they would invite him.

'Be careful over that crack in the floor,' some joker added. 'Do you want an extra cushion?

'Drinking already, so little and yet so experienced –'

'Not so little where it counts!'

It was also, no doubt, the alcohol, which Pavlik never refused. He did not talk much when he was drunk, but took to sloping wordlessly along the corridors, clenching and unclenching his fists. The tendons on his neck stood out. He, who had been so peaceable, became angry. Arguments flared up with his roommates: they were keeping him awake, encroaching on his part of the room. He stopped taking showers and grew a tufty, gingery ghost of a beard.

One day a girl from one of Pavlik's classes dropped by to borrow a book, and he offered her tea. It was the dead time in the middle of the afternoon and soon there was a small group in the corridor marvelling loudly at Pavlik's way with women, the little devil. The girl did not stay long, and once she had left, Pavlik came out into the corridor with a bottle in his hand, opening his mouth to shout at them. No sound came out. Then he dropped the bottle and left the hostel, returning, very drunk, at midnight.

There were apologies the next day. No one really wanted to hurt Pavlik; it was just that we were all cooped up together, bored and thoughtless. From then on the boys exerted themselves to be friendly, but he was never convinced. His eyes, circled by purplish shadows, flickered warily over them and went blank: as he'd expected, they didn't really mean it.

In that blank look I saw disillusion. So this is real life, he seemed to be saying. This is what I bore those years in the children's home for, what I stifled my complaints and starved for. All those years you promised me that one day I would leave the institution and be a Soviet citizen, like everyone else. All lies. No one is a Soviet citizen now. Each one of us is alone, each of us is orphaned.

Pavlik cut the arteries in his wrists soon afterwards. When Mitya and I came back from the cinema, there was a kerfuffle in the corridor and the *Komendant* was shouting 'Open, open up, idiot!' and heaving his shoulder against Pavlik's door. We leant our shoulders to the task and the door burst open. Inside Pavlik was lying on his bed smiling faintly. Blood was running down his hands and soaking into his mattresses. Seeing us, he picked up the razor and began to saw at his wounds.

'Leave me,' he whispered.

He screamed as they dragged him down the corridor, and the noise hung in the air long after he had gone. We wiped the stains on his bed half-heartedly and avoided each other's eyes. Then Viktor announced, 'Son of a bitch, I'm thirsty,' and we turned to him in noisy agreement. We sat in Viktor's room that night.

Pavlik didn't stay long in hospital, but by the time he returned, his possessions had been moved to a room on a different floor. We saw little enough of him after that. From glimpses in the corridor, I noticed that Pavlik had shaved off his beard and begun to grow a moustache; it aged him. A little later, two friends appeared in his life and the three of them played table tennis together. Pavlik seemed to be surviving, yet when we had first met him, only a few months before, you could watch the emotions following one another across his features: fear and boredom and half-credulous hope. Now his face had settled into a single expression: the aggressive stare that had formerly seemed comic. Don't think me sad because I am alone in the world, it seemed to say. I've grown strong, because I rely only on myself. You are weak: you need each other. But one day you will know what I know: each of us is alone, each of us is an orphan . . .

· 13 ·

Inflation Fever

Like Boris Yeltsin in a television interview last week, Mr Gorbachev gave a warning of 'unpopular, but necessary' economic measures to come, but neither he nor his economic advisers would elaborate on what they had in mind.

The Times, 22 October 1991

Here comes trouble: open the gates wide!

Russian proverb

That winter I learnt a new skill: walking on icy pavements. It's not as simple as it sounds. Each step must be deliberate, flat-footed, like a prison warder – no lazy, sweet swing of the hips. The bones of the pelvis, which in spring jut forward away from the curve of the spine, in winter disappear back into the flesh. The centre of balance must be held exactly above the feet. The eyes must be fixed on the ground to verify each foothold, the arms must hover out from the body ready to save you if all else fails. And in my case, there was no guarantee that any of this would save me; the more careful I was, it seemed, the more capriciously the ground shot from beneath me and the bus stop reappeared upside down, with a hand of Mitya's reaching from the sky to haul me up once he could stop laughing.

It was a slippery time altogether. As the temperature continued to fall, the curtains opened on a series of magic tricks that astonished us all. The world turned white and familiar shapes were shrouded. A man in a suit conjured up all the kopecks in the country and pfff! made them disappear. A one-rouble note wrapped in a handkerchief became ten roubles, then twenty-five, then one hundred, then five hundred, and finally – drum roll – one thousand roubles! As a finale, an assistant wheeled a casket on stage that contained savings accounts, hundreds of thousands of them. The audience trembled as, with a silver sword, he sliced them in half! And in quarters! And at last each little nest egg hatched into a rook and flew away. The show ran and ran: they called it hyperinflation.

Alchemy of a sort occurred that year. Even the poor became millionaires. They sold their watches and their televisions and took home wads of roubles instead. Wallets couldn't hold all their money. They stuffed their pockets full of notes, bought Polish plastic bags to carry the loot. At first they found it hard to throw off their old-style thriftiness. They took their crisp new notes home, stashed them away with their valuables and papers, and in no time the value had evaporated and all that was left was paper. Soon we began to realise that the only sensible way to manage our personal finances was to spend like one-armed bandits. The faster the coins disappeared, the more chance you had of hitting the bonus button. As long as you were winning, it was exhilarating.

Rules for Hyperinflationary Times

1. Spend now, worry later. Never be cautious. Spend more than you earn: that way you'll get rich. And never leave your savings in the bank. Blow it all on fur coats and televisions.
2. Don't expect your employer to pay you. Don't expect your employees to turn up every day. And by the way, job security is dead. You're sacked.
3. If you are a professional musician, film director, scientist, soldier, coal miner, steelworker or academic, you'd better adapt, or starve. Forget your training. Forget, above all, your career. Don't produce anything. Don't get involved in manual labour. Import–export is the only way to keep your head above water. Buy and sell. Buy and sell. The faster the better.
4. Legal work does not make money, thus the simple equation: a successful person is a criminal.
5. In all, rely only on dollars. Not the state, employers, friends, lovers. Dollars are the only real certainty.

The first time I had changed money in Voronezh, back in September, the exchange gave me several packs of new-issue twenty-five-rouble notes, purplish-mauve with the curvy, curly lettering that you expect on circus posters. There were then thirty-nine roubles to the dollar, and the average monthly pension was forty-two roubles. The money came to us still bound in wads of a hundred notes; Emily and I broke one open, took half each and went to the market.

It was not long since the official exchange rate had been one rouble to one pound, and some of the prices in the shops were still fixed on that basis – not essentials, but goods that had been manufactured under the old system and sold slowly: a pair of ice skates for forty-two roubles, for example, a cheese grater for six. The sense of how much a currency is worth does not disappear instantly: in the public perception, at least, the rouble was still worth something like one pound. Imagine this hapless foreigner asking for six apples – and pulling out of her pocket a whole stack of huge, spanking new purple twenty-five-pound notes. The stall owner looked at me with a sort of horror, and shook her head.

'Impossible! I haven't change for that sort of money.' She shoved an apple into my hands and said, '*Vozmi, i vita-miniziruisya!* Take this and vitaminise yourself!' And she turned to bawl at her scrawny little husband, for no reason other than the trick that was being played with her livelihood.

Some of the trade was still controlled by the central planners. I imagined them up in Moscow, totting up rows of figures on an abacus. 'So . . .' they'd say, jotting something down. 'One rubber boot costs ten roubles and seventy kopecks, and a pair for twenty-one roubles forty.' The prices were like that, precise to the last kopeck. Forty-three roubles and twelve kopecks for a saucepan, one hundred and eight roubles and nineteen kopecks for a plane ticket. A marketing manager would have blanched; the thought cheered me as I searched for change with numb fingers and the queues buckled and muttered behind me. There was a brass dish beside the cash register to receive the money, and the shop assistants had a way of tapping on it and breathing heavily through their noses that was guaranteed to make you scatter your coins on the floor.

In Soviet times, the fixed price for a piece of bread in a café was one kopeck, and a glass of tea, I believe, cost three. Anywhere in the Union you could be sure of a modest snack for ten kopecks; that hadn't changed since the war. That winter, the kopeck quietly vanished from circulation. Once we reached a hundred roubles to the dollar or so, there was no point. The only ones that remained, and in fact rose in value with inflation, were the *dvushki*, the two-kopeck pieces, which you needed for public telephones. Enterprising babushkas sold stacks of them outside the central post office: ten two-kopeck pieces for twenty roubles.

As Christmas approached, a vivid green note began to circulate, the colour of birch leaves as they push their way out of the bud. It was worth a hundred roubles. The girl at the exchange could not help shaking her head as she counted them out to me, two for each tatty dollar. Mitya and I decided to eat – I was feeling as though the ground was far away, as though the notes stuffed in my pockets made me lighter, more buoyant.

The nearest shop was the Gastronom by the station, a dirty place where we had once seen a rat running along the eye-level shelves behind the shop assistant's head. Usually there was a bustle of housewives, alcoholics cringing at the vodka counter, the ordinary crowd. That day the place was empty, apart from a single assistant who was humming in the corner. Her voice echoed tunelessly in the huge, columned hall. It was not simply that there were no customers. The shelves, yards and yards of them looping gracefully along the curving wall, were bare. In one of the counters there was a display of bread made of plaster; the bread racks behind stood unused. I fingered the crisp birch-leaf notes in my pocket and shivered.

The assistant called us over. 'The only products we have today are these,' she told us, and waved at the shelves behind her. There was a row of green and silver bottles.

Champagne, from the Moscow champagne factory – *sek* or *demi-sek* (as we say in Russian). Either one cost the same: about seventy pence.

'It was meant to be here for New Year,' the assistant said nonchalantly. 'Just arrived last week. And chocolate bars, if you want. Not cheap, though.'

Beneath the champagne lay a pile of familiar black and red wrappers: Mars bars.

Mitya and I sat on a bench outside the shop and started in. It's interesting how champagne drunk of necessity has a different effect. No aristocratic jollity for us. We were drunk, of course, but it was a sober drunkenness, a light-headed, yet solemn state.

'So we'll live on champagne and chocolate alone,' said Mitya.

'Better than the French Revolution,' I agreed, beginning to nod and then deciding against it.

The bubbles ran to my head, and it was not long before I was feeling so buoyant that I had to hold onto the seat with both hands.

The Uvarovs had the first five-hundred-rouble note that I came across. It was larger, with the swirly writing this time in piercing fuschia pink – really the prettiest bank note I have seen. I dropped in to see them just after they'd withdrawn their savings from the bank.

'Come in, come in,' Mrs Uvarov said kindly, as always. 'You look dreadful. Have something to eat with us, come along.'

I ate a bowl of soup while they planned how best to spend the money. It was at about this time that I remember hearing a calculation on the radio: if you bought a tonne of steel in Russia, sold it for foreign currency, and then spent that foreign currency on Russian steel; if this were possible, and you repeated the operation just eight times, you could buy the entire Russian steel industry.

This was a hypothetical exercise, of course, but all the same, millions were being made that year. Everyone had something that they were trying to sell abroad, and in the Uvarovs' case, it was an enormous petrified log. I don't know how they had come by such a thing, but they were confident that there was a living to be made from it. They were ringing up, writing letters, spending every evening driving about all over the place to talk to people about the log.

It's a strange thing, considering how lazy everyone knows Russians to be. Sloth, which wraps the gentry in their dressing gowns and sends the peasant to doze on his stove, has long been recognised as a part of the national character. Yet that winter people took on two or three extra jobs as well as their regular employment. They became taxi drivers, businessmen, antique dealers and speculators in currency. In the evenings they arrived home late, having driven twenty miles out of town to collect a spare part for the Lada which an acquaintance had agreed to exchange for a pair of fur boots. In the mornings they dropped in on a friend who was willing to sell dollars at a slightly lower rate, then picked up a passenger and ferried him to the other end of town before arriving at work, again late. Arriving on time at work was a luxury that even the most punctual couldn't afford that winter. And yet they still arrived at the office somehow, despite the fact that their salaries shrunk each day and often were not paid for three or four months.

And not only did they work hard, they took risks and responded to the market. Everyone became an entrepreneur, gambling their savings on a load of Turkish fruit juice, or Polish cigarettes that they then tried to sell on. As salaries were delayed by month upon month, workers began to accept payment in the goods they produced. Along the big highways the rows of figures sitting quietly beside identical piles of saucepans (if theirs was a saucepan factory), or buckets, or even garden gnomes became common. How did they survive? Mr Uvarov laughed when I asked him.

'How do any of us survive?' he replied, shrugging. 'Habit, I suppose.'

It's rare, I suspect, for people to come to Russia in search of moderation. When I arrived my head was stuffed so full of preposterous excesses, it made my eyes bulge. I'd read, for instance, that at the court of Nicholas II, so many jewels were pouring out of Siberia that they didn't content themselves with necklaces. Collars, belts, whole breastplates of diamonds became the fashion. In the nineteenth century, the Tolstoys were so particular about their laundry that they sent it to be washed in Holland. As 1917 unravelled, the last aristocrats in the Empire washed their hair in champagne and danced barefoot in troughs of caviar. A few months later most of them were penniless or dead, but the attitude lived on. As late as 1982, the Communist Party leader in Azerbaijan, Geidar Aliyev, had an entire palace built for a visit by Brezhnev and presented him with a monstrous ring, which consisted of one large jewel (representing the Soviet Union, under Brezhnev) surrounded by fifteen smaller ones (the Soviet Republics). Brezhnev stayed for the weekend; the palace was not used again.

Yakov had inherited something of this spirit, heaven knows

where from. In the New Year he and Nina parted ways. Nina had grown tired of listening to Yakov improvise on his guitar, and Yakov had begun to look hunted. He became very thin and seemed to develop a horror of physical contact. One evening I caught his expression of disgust as he glanced down at her hand holding his. They agreed to end the affair and Yakov did not visit the hostel for some weeks. Nina was a phlegmatic girl, and the entire episode – the turbulent opening scenes, the anguish, though short-lived, of her friend, Liza Minelli, and the anticlimactic end – barely impinged on her manner of faintly vacuous cheer. Soon the three girls were lolling in bed together until afternoon, drinking tea and stubbing cigarettes out in old beer cans, the same as ever. Yakov, however, seemed badly shaken.

The next time I saw him it was three o'clock on a chill February morning and he was leaning over my bed, shaking me by the shoulder. Emily and Ira slept on.

'Come down to the station with me. I want to show you something.'

I sat up. 'What –'

'Come on, let's go to the station.' He was trembling. The half-light from the corridor emphasised his thinness, his puffy eyes.

'OK, let me get dressed.' It occurred to me that I'd rather he did not go down to the station alone. He had an air of urgency that felt dangerous.

Yakov and I walked out into the black, glittering street. The temperature was a steady ten degrees below and the wind had fallen. At night, the ice compelled even the clouds far above to be still. Only the breath rising from our lips like blue feathers defied it.

Yakov led me through the station and up the iron stairs of a bridge over the tracks. I clattered behind him. He hadn't spoken since we left the hostel. Now he stopped in the centre of the bridge, panting, and waited. It was a fine, solid, Soviet construction, covered, with sides five foot high and crisscross wire netting stretched above, so no one could come to harm on the tracks. Where we stood, a long jag in the wire had been cut open and the loose section bounced gently, shaken by our footsteps. I waited with Yakov, watching him out of the corner of my eye. We were both shivering.

A torchlight was wavering towards us along the rails; the ringing note of iron against iron identified it as a signalman, checking the points. As he drew closer I saw him puffing as he walked, bending and swinging his hammer rhythmically.

'That must be a lonely life,' I remarked to break the silence.

It struck a nerve. Yakov responded in a high, wobbly voice. 'Yes, you know I work and I study . . . struggle to do the best for everyone . . . and the whole world is running and no one has time . . . even my mother hardly speaks to me since I came back from Minsk . . . and all these people, my friends, these girls – they all want something from me and I'm exhausted, given my heart and yet rejected . . .'

'But Yakov, what do you mean? You haven't been to visit us lately, we thought you must be too busy. I heard you were working?'

'I have been! Working like a madman, and yet what comes of it but problems, awkwardnesses?' Yakov paced away from me and back. He was very pale, on the verge of tears. 'You know what, if this was a stage and down there –' he gestured at the tracks – 'down there were ten thousand people – *ten thousand* – waiting and watching, you know what I'd say to them?' He expanded his chest. 'I would stand here, and I would say, "None of you, not a single one of you understands me."'

There was a pause. After a moment I couldn't help myself; a bubble of laughter rose in my throat and burst. 'Come on,' I said hurriedly. 'We are your friends, dear Yakov, whatever you think. Let's go back. It's too cold.'

Yakov nodded, deflated. He left me at the door of the hostel and went home.

A few days later I heard the rest of the story. The Salvation Army were setting up a branch in Voronezh and for some reason they had employed Yakov to install their telephone system for them. Why, the Lord only knows: Yakov was a mysterious answer to their prayers. He was hardly an electronics expert, although that was not the real problem.

The awkwardness emerged when the Salvation Army called Yakov in and spread half a million roubles on the table before him. Money for equipment, they told him. No doubt they arranged a date by which the system would be ready. Perhaps they suggested convenient times for installation, when the office would be empty. Being Christian soldiers, uninterested in money, they did not notice the expression on

Yakov's face as he gazed at half a million roubles in brand-new notes. He'd never seen so much money before. He pocketed it and walked out of the building in a daze. Nina and he were no longer going out, but he'd met a girl the week before, a beautiful girl, she'd been on his mind ever since. She'd been visiting, but now she'd be back in her home in Minsk. Yakov found himself down by the station. Minsk, Minsk – there was a train in several hours' time. Ah, to hell with it, he thought, and got in a taxi.

'Take me to Minsk,' he announced, spilling half a million roubles onto the leatherette seats. Then he fell asleep and dreamt he was swimming in warm water.

In Minsk, one thousand kilometres later, they waited for some hours outside an empty flat. Late that night, the girl came home with her boyfriend. She was less than pleased to find Yakov and the taxi driver, who happened to be called Brezhnev, on her doorstep. She let them stay the night on her floor, however, and cooked them fried eggs in the morning.

'Pretty girl,' said Brezhnev approvingly, when they left the flat after breakfast. 'So, chief, time to go home?'

Four days after the meeting with the Salvation Army, Yakov arrived back in Voronezh. Brezhnev dropped him off at the station.

'Mind if I leave you here, boss? You've worn me out with this trip of yours. I'm going home. My wife'll give me hell! She'll never believe that I've been to Minsk and back . . . Oh, here's your change, colonel. Take it and good health to you!'

He pressed fifty thousand roubles into Yakov's hand and drove away.

Apart from his midnight visit, I didn't see Yakov for a time. The Salvation Army were understanding, I heard, and even carried on employing him. Perhaps they saw him as a prodigal son, although Yakov was not repentant. According to him, he had been spreading love in the world. It was just that we did not understand him.

I continued to feel dizzy and light-headed, and after a couple of weeks Mitya arranged for me to see his doctor. The waiting room was full and silent. Even the children were subdued. An old lady was crying as she talked to the receptionist. Now and again a sob broke from her, and she repeated, 'He'll kill me! If I go back, he'll kill me!'

'We can't help you here, *babulya*, forgive us,' the receptionist said firmly.

I was beckoned into the doctor's room at last, where she tapped my chest and asked me staccato questions. When she'd finished, she sighed, and sat down.

'Half the population of this city is suffering from dizziness,' she said shortly. 'They're not eating enough fruit and vegetables, they're not sleeping properly, their nerves are in a state of agitation, they're exhausted. It's the life we're living these days. Just try and take better care of yourself, *ladno*?'

A final example of inflation fever: Arkady left Voronezh before I arrived, headed for Moscow and found a job in a brand-new casino. I heard a lot about him, though, how he was working as a croupier, how he was promoted to one of the tills. Once he came down to visit, a lanky man with indecisive features. He described the casino to us matter-of-factly, the owners in three-piece suits, the punters with their blondes, security who gave a guy brain damage the week before. (He'd been messing about with the croupier, a girl. If it had been anything more serious they'd have killed him.) He seemed to me to be unimpressed by it all.

Impressed or otherwise, however, it made no difference. For Arkady was a gambler. One quiet afternoon, when the owners were out, Arkady put eight thousand dollars from his till into a carrier bag, walked to a casino where no one knew him, played – with a look on his face as though he was slipping in and out of sleep – and lost it all. They caught it all on closed-circuit TV. Then he disappeared.

Eight thousand dollars was not a great deal for the owners of a casino in Moscow, particularly then, when the Russians flocked joyfully to the tables as though the times demanded it. But they would not let anyone rob them and go unpunished. They searched, and when, after a few weeks, they did not find him, they sent someone to drop in on Arkady's parents in Voronezh.

'You'll have to pay us back,' he told them. 'Plus interest.'

Arkady's parents were elderly. They'd moved to Voronezh when they retired and now they were living on their pensions. So his father found a job as a watchman, and told the casino owners that they would pay them back, a few dollars a month. Don't worry, he said proudly, you'll get your money.

But the casino owners were not happy with the arrangement. Again they sent their man to Voronezh.

'I said, you'll have to pay us back,' he told them again. 'Not some miserable few dollars a month. Now.'

And he smashed up the place a bit, so that they understood. They sold their flat and paid off the debt. Then they rented a room in a communal apartment, where they live still. They suffer from the lack of privacy and the cockroaches, but they suffer most for the loss of their son. Arkady has never reappeared, although there was a rumour that he'd gone to Amsterdam; others say he's still in Moscow, hiding; others that he's dead.

· 14 ·

The Commission Shop

I started going out again at night in February. It was dark by half past four and once the offices had emptied, the streets were soon quiet. The atmosphere in the city had changed since the autumn, when Mitya and I had walked all evening. Now there were stories of muggers, and a friend of ours had been set upon by a group of drunken teenagers – young boys – and beaten up. I carried a tiny canister of Mace and only told Emily where I was going. Russians would just have made a fuss and tried to stop me.

With my hood up and a scarf covering half my face against the cold, I ran out of the hostel gates, through the First of May Park opposite, and across Petrovsky Square. Just past the statue of Peter the Great, I turned down a steep little alley and arrived at an iron door. My knock sounded too loud; I restrained myself from looking over my shoulder. An eye appeared at the peephole, and in a second filled with the jangle of padlock and bolts I was suddenly certain I'd walked into a trap. Then Mitya opened the door, grinning.

'Look at this,' he said instantly, pulling me inside. 'There's a jacuzzi – Chinese crisps – and here, food for cosmonauts!'

Mitya had taken on a night watchman's job in a commission shop to earn some extra money. It made him the envy of many; not only was it unusual to find part-time jobs that actually paid, but he could spend all evening inspecting the strange and exotic goods that appeared on its shelves. For example, there really was spacemen's food: vacuum-packed yellow pills like dog biscuits, which described themselves as 'High-nutrition sustenance for a gravity-free environment'.

'People buy it for the vitamins,' said Mitya gleefully. 'Let's try one.'

'No –'

'OK. Let's try the Chinese crisps then. I didn't think they ate crisps in China.'

'For goodness' sake –' But he was already ripping open the packet. I don't know why I felt so nervous. It was partly that the flutter of fear as I ran through the park hadn't quite left me. But I was also wary of the owners of this shop, men who wore creaky leather jackets and looked their customers up and down with leaden aggression before serving them. They'd been drinking before they left; a couple of empty brandy bottles and three smeared glasses stood behind the counter, along with two or three videos:

Casanova in Russia, Schoolgirls' Excursion. I couldn't shake the thought that they were still there, watching Mitya make free with their property. Then I realised: the shop smelt of them, of old cigarettes and leather, overlaid by a powerful waft of aftershave.

The commission shop owners were making money that winter; they had all the right friends, who were also making money. The basic business plan was simple. You imported cheap goods from China, Poland, Romania – anywhere with an economy that was affordable – and you pegged the prices to the dollar. People still bought them. What else were they to do, if they needed a winter coat and Soviet goods had disappeared from the shops?

And there was a thrill in this random, brightly coloured array. Banana-flavoured liqueurs, books on acupuncture, marbled chocolate cakes in shiny wrappers, purple suspender belts and marital aids in the shape of Elvis Presley – no one had seen anything like it. They poured in off the sludgy February streets, out of their fusty, cracked-Formica offices and the neon-lit crush on the trolley bus that stank of mildew and sweat; they crowded in to stare at the goods and to ask, timidly, if they might inspect a pair of boots made in India with a rubber logo on the ankle saying 'Kikkers'. And in return the thug lounging against the shelves would narrow his eyes and expel a lungful of smoke in their direction, wondering whether, really, it was worth the effort to stretch his arm even the six inches necessary to fulfil their request.

'What are you looking like that for?' said Mitya, taking my hand. 'Don't worry, they've gone for the evening. Sit down, have some vodka.'

'I don't want vodka, thanks.'

'All right, have a beer. Look, here's what I'm going to get you as a present.'

In the counter was a pile of women's underwear in various colours. A daisy with huge eyes and a pink dress decorated the packets.

'They're made in North Korea,' Mitya told me. 'I bet you don't know anyone else who wears North Korean lingerie.'

I laughed. Mitya went on. 'God, they're going to be jealous! Look at this on the front of the packet: "firm support", "imparts silky texture to skin", "treated with herb medicine to increase size of ladies' chest".'

'No!'

'Yes – look. How does one know what size to buy, I wonder?'

We giggled about it, drank beer, and ate the picnic that Mitya's mother had packed up for him: black bread, sausage, and two slices of salty white *salo*, pig fat. We balanced ourselves on the broken-down sun lounger that was Mitya's bed and watched the crackly old video of *Hair* that Lapochka had lent us. And it was only much later, looking around at the shelves crowded with useless, expensive gimmicks, with plastic boxes three times as large as their contents, with piles of clothes and knick-knacks and chemical drinks, that it struck me as pitiful.

'You know what it reminds me of,' Mitya said, trying to cheer me up. 'It's what Sveta's flat will be like one day, with all her hoard stacked up all around her.'

I laughed. 'Of course! That's what she's planning. A shop selling empty shampoo bottles –'

'– and old clothes and saucepans with no handles. She'll make her fortune.'

'Yes she will, sooner or later, I'm certain.'

If this were a Soviet novel, Sveta would surely be the heroine. She carried her beauty as though it were a mild disability; if anyone stared or, in the Russian way, murmured compliments to her in the street ('Your eyebrows are the wings of birds!'), she tossed her head and tutted. The practicalities of life were her concern. She had astonishing aquamarine eyes that looked out of her smooth, high-cheeked face with a matter-of-fact expression. Her nose was pretty and her chin was determined. The abundant tawny hair that glittered in sunlight was usually scraped back into a bun, and every muscle in her sturdy body was set to work scrubbing the floor, wringing her clothes dry or slicing vegetables double-speed. She was always busy.

Only that afternoon, Emily and I had been lolling on our beds when we heard a rustling and clinking from the other end of the room. Looking closer, we found Sveta under the table collecting the empty bottles for the deposit.

'Go ahead,' we said shirtily. 'Don't mind us.'

Sveta, like most people, was concentrating on surviving

the winter. She didn't only collect bottles. Under her bed were her savings; year after year of presents and castoffs from English students which she had seized upon, cleaned, and arranged neatly in boxes. Slivers of old soap, medicines, half-used exercise books, knives and forks, all tied together with little pieces of string.

'Do you want this?' she was always asking casually, picking up a bottle of shampoo with a couple of drips left in the bottom, or an old biro. Viktor teased her that she was putting together her trousseau.

'Have me, Sveta. I can bring a knife and fork and half a towel to the union!'

But Sveta just tossed her hair back and turned away from him, smiling. She had already chosen her man. He was called Sasha, a quiet, clever boy with a soft beard who sat out in the hostel corridor. Their courtship was lengthy. Months passed while they drank tea together; Sveta's beautiful eyes glittered and Sasha blushed. This continued until even the hostel gossips lost interest. One day, however, we noticed that Sasha no longer sat in the corridor but instead in Sveta's room, having removed his shoes and left them neatly at the door. Sveta's room was always spick and span and the stirrings of passion were certainly not going to interfere with hygiene.

After this, things moved more quickly. While walking home from university one evening, Sveta spotted a job advertisement among the frillies on the lampposts. These scraps of paper had a description of the job or service offered at the top, and underneath, a fringe of small strips bearing a telephone number, ready for the interested passer-by to tear off. Most people, if they needed to sell their car or swap their flat for two smaller ones, needed to do no more than write out several dozen frillies and post them up around town. And Mr Jackson, despite being an honest-to-goodness American entrepreneur and a genuine example of the foreign investment that had arrived to transform the planned economy, used the same method to advertise the job of his assistant. Sveta was a connoisseur of the frillies and she saw straight away that this was something out of the ordinary. Within a week Sasha, in a neatly pressed suit, had applied for the post and been accepted.

A decade or so earlier, Sasha's new employer, Mr Jackson, was a millionaire businessman in Texas, when he had a dream telling him to follow the path of spirituality or die. Mr Jackson was so struck by the dream that he sold everything and went to India, where he spent seven years at the feet of a guru in the mountains. He was in his mid-seventies when the guru finally told him that only in Russia would he become truly spiritual. Upon which Mr Jackson stuck a pin in a map of the USSR and promptly began negotiations to buy a huge farm in the Voronezh region. The idea was to found a sort of Happy Valley of plenty and communal living, combining American technology with the area's rich black earth.

His plan seemed to be taking a long time to materialise.

Sasha, when questioned, would say only that it was complicated. People used to point to a house close to the University
park – a house where, according to a plaque, Tolstoy once visited his goddaughter for tea – and hiss, 'The house of Mr
Jackson!' I hoped that the ageing seeker after truth took comfort from this coincidence, for no doubt there was much in the
progress of Russian reforms that was dispiriting.

Foreign investors had otherwise shown little interest in
the city. Economic rationalisation, the process by which
Russia's rusting plant was to be refashioned into consumer
goods factories sweetly humming with activity, had not taken
off. The glittering left bank produced at least some mar-
ketable goods. In this the city was better off than many that
relied on armaments factories, like Tula; but still the
Voronezh televisions gathered dust on the conveyor belt,
waiting for the cathode tubes made in Tbilisi and circuit
boards from the Baltic states.

'You know, they call this a transitional period,' said Mr
Uvarov to me one day, bitterly. 'It's like the early twenties,
that was a transitional period too. All those Social Democrats
and Social Revolutionaries, on the same side as the Bolsheviks,
as they saw it, all working away to establish a socialist
state . . . then they were all massacred just a few years later.
They had a transitional mentality, or something. That's what
they'll say about us. "Of course, they tried, but they made
unforgivable mistakes . . . victims of the transitional period,
what could they do? It was their fate." And all the time this is
our life . . .'

There were several attempts at joint ventures with foreign companies. An Italian firm set up a pizza restaurant: installed a shiny oven, trained a couple of chefs, and left, satisfied that one more city would now have access to civilisation with extra pepperami. For some months the pizzas were cheap, tasty and fast. Mitya and I liked watching the chefs slapping the dough down onto the huge trays and sliding them into the oven. The restaurant was warm and bustling and although you could only stand at chest-high tables, it was always full. I seem to remember pontificating to Mitya about the advantages of the free market as we stood and ate.

'Oh, bla bla bla,' Mitya responded, crunching a pizza crust. We weren't getting on so well. Also I'd refused to stop for a hundred grammes of vodka on the way to the café.

Then types of pizza started dropping off the menu. The prices, of course, went up with inflation and the place began to empty. We still came, although we often had to wait ten minutes for the chef to appear behind his counter. Then the pizza dough turned grey and gritty and the toppings shrank to a smear of tomato and a few hunks of sausage. I don't know what the story was: protection money almost certainly, difficulties with supplies, low morale, and perhaps just a sort of diffusion, an atmosphere that somehow smeared itself even on that shiny oven.

The Gastronom on Revolution Prospect where we collected our sugar ration was at the other end of the diffusion process. We were given coupons for all the necessities: grain, meat, butter, eggs, household soap and one bottle of vodka a month, but it was only sugar that was strictly rationed. Picking it up at this time of year was bleak. We queued up first to show our passports and sign the register. Then we queued again, watching the assistant as she shovelled pinkish granulated sugar into bags. Her big arms were flushed with exertion and her mouth was grimly set. Bag after bag was whisked over the scales and dumped on the counter as she yelled, 'Next!'

Nearby old ladies hovered, looking mournfully at their ration and itching to weigh it again. But no one had the courage to ask. That assistant was a bully. She was capable of taking back the sugar, emptying it on the floor, and demanding 'Happy now?'

Later, economic analysts would say 'Of course, people survived that winter because they still had savings accounts stuffed with roubles, as well as the vegetables and so on from their dachas.' It was not how it felt at the time. We went on from the Gastronom to the Central Market, which was half-deserted. Most of the concrete display slabs were empty, and the pigeons fluttering and calling in the dome could be heard above the commercial bustle below. In one corner the honey vendors still beckoned, offering to dab the back of your hand with their stiff, yellow nectar. There was sour cream to buy from women wrapped and bandaged against the draughts, and on the opposite side of the hall, stringy old men in aprons were selling pairs of trotters wired together and heaps of offal flecked with sawdust. But the

toppling mounds of vegetables had dwindled away to potatoes and moon-faced cabbages, and what customers there
were only drifted between the counters, asking prices, nod-
ding, and drifting on.

In the street outside a row of pensioners stood in the cold.
They wore their best coats and hats, and at their feet lay their
prize possessions: a set of novels by Alexei Tolstoy, crystal
glasses, shiny pairs of shoes that had been wrapped in felt
since the sixties, a rug from the Caucasus. They looked
strangely diminished in the open air.

'How much would you like for the shoes?' I asked an old
lady.

'Whatever you'll give me,' she answered faintly. 'I'm a
teacher, I'm not used to this kind of thing.'

She reminded me of Lisa, the great-aunt who starved in
Moscow at the end of the twenties. In those days, too, the
middle classes had stood outside selling everything they
owned. There are photographs of pianos and chandeliers in
the snow, being snapped up by the new Soviet bourgeoisie.
Antiques in Russia do not have an easy time. Those same
chandeliers were probably back out on the street in 1992.

As March began, torpor fell on the hostel. The days were
short and dull and there was no light in the sky. We slept a lot.
Jim appeared out of his room one day looking a little dazed,
saying, 'That makes one hundred and nine hours since I last
left the hostel.' Some went travelling to shake off the sadness;
one boy left for Mount Elbrus to learn to ski. He stayed so

long that he'd qualified as a professional ski instructor by the time he returned.

Others were driven a little crazy. One of the English girls drank so much vodka that at last it poisoned her, and she lay shrieking in the corridor until a doctor arrived and gave her a shot of adrenalin. Peanut, trying to impress, kept attempting to climb up the outside of the hostel to his new girlfriend's window and failing; he gave himself a black eye and gashed his leg, and no one was sympathetic. Parties were as likely to end with a group of girls sobbing together as dancing; one was in love with a bastard, another had had an abortion, and none of us knew what we'd be doing in six months' time. The year limped towards spring.

I escaped from it all, wrapping my head in a scarf, running across the First of May Park and banging on the iron door of Mitya's shop. We spent the night there, sleeping fitfully on the sun lounger. In the mornings I was exhausted by a procession of busy, unpleasant dreams that were instantly forgotten. Only one stuck in my mind. I was standing in the stairwell of a block of flats in Voronezh. A woman opened the door to me, holding her dressing gown around herself with one hand. In the grimy light she looked fat and forty and tired of life, but she managed an ironic little smile. 'Hello,' she said. 'You don't know me.' At first it looked like Sveta, but as I woke, I realised it was me.

The shop smelt stale and claustrophobic. I dressed quietly. Mitya was still asleep as I inched open the iron door and walked out into the shadowy street.

Later that day Mitya came to the hostel to find me. He put his hands on my shoulders and looked at me searchingly.

'I've brought you something,' he said at last. 'We're going to stay together, aren't we?'

I peered inside the bag he'd given me. There lay a set of peach-coloured North Korean lingerie (size: medium).

· 15 ·

International Women's Day

On International Women's Day, I bumped into Yakov with his new girlfriend, inspecting the roses for sale in glass cases outside the station. She was called Katya, a dewy-eyed, sweet girl from Voronezh, who accepted Yakov on his own reckoning. The flower sellers were doing a busy trade; clusters of men stood waiting, counting out roubles in their hands. It was important to buy flowers for the woman in your life on 8 March. You'd never hear the end of it otherwise.

The girls in Room 99 had explained it all to me. On International Women's Day, Soviet women bask in their menfolk's love and gratitude. In the morning, as it is a holiday, they lounge in bed instead of going out to work. Their husbands, with much cursing and clattering of pans, cook breakfast for the family; by ten o'clock they proudly serve their wives a charred and shrivelled egg. Beside the woman's plate will be a bunch of flowers and a little gift, a bottle of scent perhaps, or a pair of tights, which she will exclaim over until the children, scarlet with fury, insist that their mother makes them their proper breakfast.

Later the real celebrations begin. A Soviet woman's days are usually taken up with dressing the children and taking them to school, arriving at the office on time, nipping out of work at lunchtime to buy something for dinner, and again in the afternoon – if they can sneak away without being reprimanded – to try and find cough medicine for the little one. They'll leave work on the dot of six so that they can pop into several more shops to check if there is anything good on offer, and into the market where they see some cheap eggs. They'll pay the electricity bill at the post office and collect the laundry, since they're passing; then they'll dump their shopping at home and pick up a bucket to fill up with those cheap eggs from the market. By the time their husbands have arrived home, they will have given the flat a vacuum, dusted, and put two lots of dirty clothes on to soak (always advisable if you're washing everything by hand). On International Women's Day, therefore, they go back to bed after breakfast and sleep like squirrels.

Their husbands, meanwhile, meet up with friends and express their feelings for their wives in the simplest and most sincere way they know: by drinking themselves into a stupor with toasts 'to our beloved ladies – where would we be without them?' Late at night they return home and tell their wives they love them. All in all, it's a not a bad day for the women of the former Soviet Union.

Yakov had spotted the flowers he wanted. 'Fourteen of the red carnations, please.'

'Fourteen!' exclaimed Katya, thrilled. 'But shouldn't it be one less or more?' Even numbers of flowers are given only at funerals in Russia.

'I have to give a few to the girls in Room 99,' he explained. 'There,' he said, dividing up the bunch and handing her five flowers with his warmest, sweetest smile. '*S prazdnikom*, darling.'

Katya's face fell and she was quiet as we walked to the hostel. In Room 99 we found the girls painting their nails dark orange and gossiping.

'*S prazdnikom*,' we greeted each other. Yakov passed out the carnations, three for each of the girls. 'Nina's making blini,' reported Tanya, taking the flowers for both of them and putting them on the table without much evidence of gratitude. 'They'll be ready soon, so stick around.'

'I certainly will,' said Yakov, squeezing in between Liza Minelli and Katya and draping an arm around each of them. He was in fine spirits.

Nina opened the door with one foot, talking over her shoulder. 'Tell Yuri too,' she called. 'Here, *golubki*, my doves,' she said, advancing with a full frying pan. 'Take, eat these blinis, in celebration of being a woman.'

'You too, Yakov,' added Liza, giving him a look from under her eyelashes that could have fried pancakes. Katya giggled nervously.

Yuri and Emily arrived and we covered blinis with thick

sour cream and red caviar and drank champagne, as families did all over Voronezh. Sometimes poverty is hard to measure.

After a bit Tanya started telling us about the affairs she'd had with the mafiosi when she was working as a secretary in the police department in her home town, and the six parrots in her parents' flat who were all called Gosha. Liza Minelli put on some music and began to dance Liza Minelli-style to it, still looking at Yakov, and then he told her she was tense, and took her over to the window and made her visualise a path through a sweet-scented forest, with a little breeze . . . Tanya told some story about going to the forest with Yakov that I can't remember, but that sent Emily into a fit of silent, breathless laughter, which, as always, made the rest of us laugh. And Katya sat on the bed saying nothing.

'Have some champagne,' Yuri offered. But she refused.

'Oh, give it to me,' Tanya demanded. 'I've known Katya for years, she's happy just to sit there like a cabbage.'

Katya bit her lip. 'I can't drink,' she said quaveringly, 'as Yakov knows very well. I'm having a baby.'

There was a pause. 'We haven't decided that,' said Yakov, leaving Liza Minelli by the window.

'What is there to decide? I'm not having an abortion.'

Liza Minelli glared at them both. 'You're pathetic,' she spat, and walked out.

'Well –' said Yuri into the silence. 'Let's drink to the baby. Congratulations.'

The next time I saw Katya was at the Easter service, a few

weeks later. Mitya refused to come; the new religious free-
doms had not changed the fact that he, like most Russians,
was an atheist. The church, however, was crowded with
people of all ages: from the babushkas in black who had wor-
shipped here for decades to the young women half-hidden
behind scarves, recent and passionate converts. The majority,
however, were here just for Easter, which promised to be a
spectacle. At midnight would come the great awakening; until
then the priests were still in mourning black, the candles were
extinguished, the iconostasis only gleamed modestly through
the murky light. The crowd jostled and shifted with excitement. They had dressed up and bought candles for the
service; at home a feast awaited them, with twelve toasts and
the *kulich*, a cake of sweet cream cheese the shape of a sand-
castle.

'I'd like to be baptised,' Katya said. 'Just so that I could cross
myself, you understand? I can't even cross myself if I see something nasty. I think it would be good for the baby, don't you?'

'Aren't you nervous about having a baby?'

'A little,' she confessed, frowning. 'But my mother's going
to help. We're going to live with her at the beginning.'

It was a quarter to midnight. The priests disappeared
behind the iconostasis and reappeared almost immediately in
golden robes stiff with embroidery. The Bishop of Voronezh
stepped out in front of them, his strong old face thrust forward purposefully. He lit the candles of the few people close
to the altar and, in a cloud of incense, followed by his priests,
he proceeded once around the interior of the church. The

excitement was building. The flame from the bishop's candle had by now spread from hand to hand back through the crowd; three hundred faces, lit from beneath, glowed and shone in the sudden heat. Those at the front were able to follow the priests, but where we were the crowd heaved and buckled, and twice I watched, unable to move, as a candle passed too close to a tangle of hair. Katya looked over her shoulder at me desperately.

'Help,' she whispered. She was being crushed from one side; she'd almost lost her footing. I grabbed her arm and pulled her back beside me. We grinned at each other, relieved.

The doors of the church were flung open. We passed through them and began to circle the church. Once, twice, three times. Hundreds of feet shuffled through the slush and pushed it back until the earth was revealed. Night air, the deep, slow voices of the choir and the rattling censer. At last we gathered in front of the doors where the bishop stood silent, surrounded by priests. The babushka beside me was weeping into her scarf.

Raising his arms in an embrace, the bishop cried out: *Christ is risen!*

And the crowd answered in a shout: *In truth he is risen.*

The bells jangled. The doors of the church opened and inside it was unbearably bright.

Katya and I left soon after midnight, although the service would continue until morning. As we hugged goodbye, I promised to visit her soon, to see if there was anything I could do to help. Now there was less of a crowd, I saw she had lost weight. Her brown, spaniel's eyes welling with emotion in her pale little face made me shiver. A less motherly figure would be hard to imagine.

It turned out that I was the one who needed help. A couple of days later, Mitya, Yakov and I were on a trolley bus trundling along the left bank, going to visit friends, when my head spun and everything went black. When I regained consciousness, they'd got me off the bus and were carrying me towards a small wooden house, painted green and blue and covered in snow. Katya appeared in the door, eyes wide.

'She fainted,' Mitya explained. 'Can she lie down?'

'Oh,' Katya said, looking over her shoulder. 'Mama!'

I leant against the doorframe and began to slide gently towards the floor. Mitya caught me under the elbow.

'What have you done to her?' Katya's mother demanded. 'Poor girl.'

Mitya went white. 'Nothing –'

'Bring her in, quick!'

I was aware, suddenly, of lying down on a couch. 'Just not eaten,' I tried to explain. My tongue felt swollen. 'Nothing . . .'

'Off you go, boys.' Katya's mother interrupted. 'Shoo!'

Mitya and Yakov were bundled out of the house.

'Nothing serious,' I finished to an empty room, and fell asleep.

In the darkness, I jolted awake and couldn't think where I was. Then a voice loomed mournfully from the road and I realised it had woken me.

'Charlotte!'

It was Mitya, furious at his dismissal. But as I staggered to my feet, Katya's mother appeared.

'Where are you going? Now you keep warm, you've got no slippers on, can't go wandering about.' She was at the window and calling before I could stop her. 'Go on home, Mitya! She's staying the night! She's fine! Just leave her alone!' She drew the curtains. 'Don't worry about him,' she said comfortably, tucking the blanket around me. 'He's brought you to the right person. I'm a doctor, you know. Now, put this under your arm. I want to take your temperature.'

Of course I should have demanded Mitya be allowed in. Instead, with a delicious sense of relief, I lay back, pressing the cold glass of the thermometer under my arm, and allowed her to boss me around. The house had a cosy, solid feeling unlike anywhere else I had been in Voronezh. The wallpaper had faded where the sun fell on it until the pattern was barely visible. There was a desk with a green-shaded light and a couple of armchairs with knitted rugs on the back. The room smelt of coal smoke from an old-fashioned stove in the corner.

'Good, no temperature. Just low blood pressure,' said Katya's mother briskly. 'Now, lie quietly. Here's Katya with a tonic for you.'

'You've woken up.' Katya gave me a glass of clear liquid and folded herself into the armchair opposite me. 'Mama's giving me tonics, too, for me and the baby.'

'What's in it?'

'Oh, vitamins, iron, natural extracts that are health-giving. Mama makes them up herself.'

A tiny, bent old lady appeared, shuffling determinedly towards one of the armchairs. She sat down and leant forward to peer at me.

'She's the English girl,' she stated. 'Well, she doesn't look well at all. Natasha was right to keep her here. She's been living an unhealthy life, like you, Katya.'

'Babushka, she does understand Russian, you know.'

Her grandmother looked unconvinced. 'What's her name?'

'Charlotte,' I answered.

'Ah, Charlotte Brontë!'

This was the usual Russian response to my name. We smiled at each other politely, then she took out the beginnings of something tiny and pale blue on her knitting needles and fell silent.

'What about your father? Where is he?' I asked Katya

'Oh, he left years ago . . . We're a house of women here, my grandmother, my mother and I. And now the baby.' Katya laughed, a breathy little giggle. 'We all think she's sure to be a girl.'

'What about dinner, Katyusha?' said her grandmother. 'Your mother's tired and your guest must eat something.'

'It's in the oven, babushka. I'll go and check.'

Katya's mother returned and felt my forehead with a cool hand. Then she sat down at her desk and began quietly writing out reports in copperplate script. The warmth and the click of the knitting needles were soporific; in this comfortable industry there was a peace that, it seemed to me, could last for generations.

It was here, in this strict, kindly matriarchy, that the Revolution breathed its last breath. The Revolution, with its images of muscly warriors, its glorification of ferocity, violence, and what it deemed the necessary spilling of blood, was a masculine affair. The old regime was feminine: weak, decadent, with soft white hands unused to work. El Lissitzky's contemporary poster, 'Beat the Whites with the Red Wedge', demonstrated this contrast graphically: a white circle – a large, soft, feminine shape – was split open by the Bolsheviks' red phallus. Propaganda constantly reinforced this idea: it was the battle of the sexes transposed onto class.

Now all those slab-chested images were lying in the snow and the red wedge had shrivelled almost to nothing. The Revolution had failed, and Russian men were faltering with it. Oh, it was still the women who came back from work and shouldered the whole burden of looking after the family. They still suffered an average of seven abortions because of the lack of other birth control; and a beaten wife was still barely an exception. But it was the men who were dying. Young men died on their military service, in fights on the street, in car crashes, in or out of prison. Middle-aged men fell ill, went into hospital, and as Gogol put it, 'got better like flies'. They were crushed by alcohol and despair. What life was left, after all, for a cosmonaut without a space programme, a statistician working with false numbers, or an unemployed Hero of Socialist Labour?

At home, however, the women rarely lost faith in the same way. Perhaps it was simply that they could not afford to with children to look after. They concentrated on the basic elements of survival: food, warm clothes, health. Within this framework, the collapse of socialism was hardly a surprise: mothers had seen it coming for twenty years, as they stood in the milk queue. And they were prepared for it, in the sense that they were prepared for any new hardship that the regime might ordain for them. Inside their apartments family life would carry on regardless: mustard plasters would be applied to chesty coughs, draughts would be rigorously excluded, a sore throat would be treated with a spoonful of honey. It made sense to me now that Katya had the courage to have the baby: it would be safe here. Yakov and others like him could come and go; they would always be marginal. They might drink too much, run off, have affairs, and even then the women had their defence: it would not be unexpected.

After a while, Katya announced that the meal was ready and we went into the kitchen to eat. I was still feeling weak and made little progress with a large plate of *kotlyety*, fried potatoes and carrot.

The grandmother watched me, murmuring without pause, 'Eat up, eat up.'

Katya's mother intervened. 'I think it's best if she does not have too much. Her stomach is not strong.'

The grandmother stopped her chorus for a moment and looked distrustfully at her daughter. Then she turned back to me. 'Eat up, eat up a little more,' she said again, 'and then I'll read your cards for you.'

'Babushka reads the cards for the whole neighbourhood,' Katya told me. 'They come and consult with her about every-thing – whether they should get married, or move, or whatever. They bring her presents –'

'They think I've got powers,' said the grandmother, smiling. 'And have you?'

'*Bozhe moi*, what a question. It's not for me to say. But I have known some witches in my time . . . The old lady, Valentina Sergeevna, do you remember her, Katya? She died last year. In her nineties, she was, and weak as a feather, but she wouldn't die . . . Week after week she lay in her bed barely eating a thing and those black eyes of hers burning. Everyone was telling her daughter, don't feed her! But she kept on giving her little pieces of chocolate. "She doesn't want to die, her daughter said to me, look at her eyes." And at the last moment, when she felt death lying down beside her, she crawled away! So weak she could barely lift her arm, and yet her daughter found her on the other side of the room under the table. And when she tried to carry her back to bed the old lady fought her and cried, and so she made her up a bed and Valentina Sergeevna died right there, under the table . . . That's a real witch, that's how strong they are.'

There had always been rumours of witches, but these days some even practised openly. Just the other day, a friend of Mitya's had discovered six needles stuck in his door and realised that his problems were caused by black magic. So he went to see a witch. As he joined the queue outside her flat, she appeared at the door, nose twitching.

'There's one of you,' she said, 'who is surrounded by evil forces of great power.' Spotting Mitya's friend, she called him up. 'You! You need my help more than anyone.'

He glowed with pride as he told us about it. It was expensive, he told us earnestly, but well worth it.

The Soviet regime never managed to crush Orthodoxy in Russia. It had still less impact on older, less articulate, but almost universally held beliefs. Lighting candles in front of the old, dark-eyed icons and circling the church three times at Easter was a part of them; also crossing yourself at the sight of a black cat, not putting empty bottles on the table, and a hundred other precautions and charms for shoring up the corners of the world. There were both male and female ministers of this faith: witches and healers and horoscope casters and herbalists. But it was usually the women who preserved it at home, combining it with a mass of traditional remedies to keep their family safe from harm. And there is no doubt that it gave comfort. It represented, among other things, a rare continuity in Russian life.

'And I can tell you who you were in a former life,' the grandmother added. 'Just eat up a few mouthfuls more.'

'I'd like that,' I replied, responding to the expectant, kind faces that surrounded me, although – superstitiously – I've always avoided having my fortune told.

Back in the sitting room, the grandmother laid out nine cards in three rows of three. 'Here's your past,' she said, patting the first row. 'Here's a great sadness, a death, followed by a long journey. Am I right?'

I nodded.

'Here you are now,' she patted the next row. 'A dark-haired young woman, and you have an important decision to make. A painful decision. There are two paths ahead of you, and a powerful force is urging you down the wrong one.'

'What sort of a decision?'

'It's about a man, isn't it?' interrupted Katya's mother. 'He's no good for her.'

'I believe it is,' pronounced the grandmother. 'You must be strong. You must think of your family, your home – here is the card for the home – and you must decide what is best for you. But if you choose the right path, look, success awaits you. Here is the card for fortune . . .'

'Russian men are not worth the suffering, Charlotte,' said Katya's mother, sighing. 'Take my word for it.'

For a moment fury prevented me from answering. How dare they try to influence me against Mitya?

'Very enlightening,' I muttered at last. 'So who was I in a former life?'

The grandmother made a series of calculations. 'You lived about 1725,' she said, 'in Mexico. A woman, a singer or a dancer.'

'A Mexican dancer!' I couldn't help laughing angrily. 'I've never heard anything so silly.'

'That's right,' she smiled. 'An entertainer, rather second-rate.'

'How funny! A second-rate entertainer!' Katya repeated delightedly. 'Performing in some bar –'

The room suddenly felt stifling. 'Thank you very much for all your kindness,' I said, standing up. 'I think I'm well enough to go back to the hostel now.'

'Are you sure? I think you should stay the night –'

'No, no, there's no need.' I had my coat on; they were following me to the door.

'In my previous life I was apparently a priestess in Ancient Egypt,' Katya's mother said. 'Well, visit us again soon –'

'Yes, look after yourself,' the grandmother called after me as I reached the street. 'Russian men need Russian girls to manage them. You'll see what I mean.'

'Goodbye, goodnight.' I'd escaped; the dark, glittering night and the cool air felt good. What did she know anyway, the interfering old woman? Her spiel was nothing but platitudes – the very worst sort, that have a ring of truth. I thought about going to the commission shop to find Mitya. But by the time I reached Friedrich Engels Street, my head was spinning again. The lights of the hostel and even the *vakhtersha*'s mealy-mouthed smile felt like a homecoming.

· 16 ·

The Thaw

Finally, there is Soviet man, the most important product of the past 60 years. . . . This is a man who, while an ardent patriot, has been and will always remain a consistent internationalist.

L. I. Brezhnev, addressing the Twenty-fifth Congress of the Soviet Communist Party, 1980

Fifty Russian families a day are arriving in Voronezh from the former Soviet republics.

Voronezh Courrier, 25 March 1992

In April the thaw began. For a fortnight it was cloudy and dull; the sky weighed on the city and people took to their beds. 'The pressure,' they said. 'It gives me a nervous headache.' An easterly wind blew; it whipped around raw corners and slid inside my collar like a knife edge against the skin. I hadn't felt so cold in all the five months of winter.

Branches and tree trunks turned black and shiny and parts of roofs started to appear. Every day for a week, snow fell, wet, sloppy drifts that soaked through fur boots and stood on the streets in puddles up to a foot deep. Walking would have been impossible if paths had not evolved, built collectively, piece by piece: hop onto that little stone, then to the kerb past the puddle, then one foot on that bit of board and a quick splash in the icy water before you reach dry land for another five yards. It was pitiful to watch the pensioners trying to follow these courses.

One day I stood on the hostel steps gazing at the pale sunshine on the poplar trees and listening to the sound of dripping water. The thrill was almost erotic.

'During my first year of military service,' Mitya said as we sat in my room drinking tea, 'in the Urals, a roar like tanks coming at us started up and for two days we all wandered around half-crazy from the noise. Then one lunch time we heard what sounded like gunfire, round after round of it. We ran down to the river and it was the ice cracking. Great chunks the size of a car were flying up in the air, rolling and crashing and roaring like an avalanche. That's what happened when it began to thaw out there.'

The atmosphere in the hostel was still subdued. Sveta was sweeping cockroaches out of her room and watching them scuttle through the doors on either side and over Mamonov's legs; he was sitting in the passage, groaning to himself, hoping for someone to drink with. Ibrahim's hapless friend came knocking at his door: Bang-bang-bang! Ibrahim! Bang-bang-bang! Ibrahim, our Syrian neighbour, never answered this cry, which echoed hoarsely down our corridor several times a day.

The outside world seldom impinged on our little community. We occasionally saw the news, less often read the papers, and ignored the stirrings on Russia's southern border. In Georgia, refugees were pouring out of Abkhazia, and up in the mountains of Karabakh, Armenians on one side and Azeris on the other were cleaning their weapons after the winter lull: we knew this, vaguely, and yet the idea that it could end in war seemed as distant and incredible as summer.

'When the weather is changing one has to be very careful of one's health.'

It was Viktor, of course, with an open bottle of vodka, saying, 'Time for *otdykh*.'

With him was one of the Armenians, Ashot, who had a face like a boy's: slight, with heavy-lidded eyes and a sleepy expression. It looked as though the two of them had already been drinking. Ashot raised his glass and said without smiling, 'To the friendship of nations.'

'Drink up,' insisted Viktor. 'Moskovskaya vodka, full of vitamins.'

Mitya was still thinking about the army. 'God, the filth we drank,' he groaned. 'When I was called up, we were taken to Kiev for registration. The first night we drank *samogon* – I thought I would die. Anyway, one boy disappeared. They didn't find him until the next morning – he'd gone to the latrines and the seat had given way beneath him. He almost drowned. There was a thousand-litre tank underneath, he had to keep swimming all night. He was so nervous, they sent him straight home –'

I had not eaten since morning, and so after two shots I noticed that the objects and people around me were brighter and clearer than they had been. The smoke from Mitya's cigarette curled upwards in fascinating bluish strands, Viktor's face was a fiery pink, and he was telling a long story about a journey to the Caucasus. I could barely understand him.

'. . . hounds . . .' he seemed to be saying. '. . . the Southern nights . . . exotic fruits, the silky moustaches of the women . . .'

Ashot leant forward. His eyelids weighed more heavily on his eyes than ever and something in his expression woke me. 'Now they are starving there. My family live in Karabakh. They've had no electricity for more than a year. They've hardly any food and no medicine and any day the Russians might drive them out of their villages or the Azeris shoot them . . . I've had no news from them since January.'

There was a pause. 'You Armenians started the war,' said Viktor.

'We have the right to freedom, just as you do.' Ashot spoke quietly.

Mitya put on his coat. 'I have to go home. My parents will be waiting for me.'

Ashot got up with him. ''Bye,' he said. 'Thanks for the warming.'

'*Nichevo.*' When they'd gone, Viktor sighed and filled our glasses. 'Back in 1988, in the army, everyone used to talk about independence. We thought it sounded wonderful. I suppose we never thought it would happen.' He drained his glass and began to tell me about the army.

Men didn't talk about their military service much. Oh, occasionally we heard about the drinking, their friends, the having to get out of bed and ready in forty-five seconds. But that day Viktor wanted to talk. 'You know they beat me until I cried,' he started. He shook his head, barely able to believe it. 'Cried! My mother always said she'd never seen me cry, yet under their boots it didn't take long.'

Viktor was sent to a base beyond the Urals, near the Chinese border – a spot that even Russians considered remote. The officers had been there so long that they'd become naturalised into two types: a few brutes, and many poor mangy creatures. When the conscripts got food parcels from home, you could be sure the latter would turn up in the dormitory on the off-chance. 'Hey guys, what's new?' they'd ask casually.

Of course it was the brutes that ran the place, along with the second-year conscripts – not the men about to go home, who wore their caps on the back of the head and lolled at their posts, chewing their cigarette butts and gazing with lofty amusement at the rest. They were separate; their imminent freedom came off them like steam. No, the men to watch were those who'd just made it into their second year, who still smarted with the treatment they'd received in the previous twelve months. They were the ones who organised entertainments like the silver chair: take three new boys and make them crouch over a seat of needles standing up in wax until their thigh muscles give way.

Four years after Viktor returned to Voronezh he went to

the doctor with a painful boil on his calf. It was lanced, and the doctor was astonished to find a needle poking out of the flesh. Over the years, it had worked its way down the leg. The doctor said he was lucky: it could just as easily have turned inwards.

For his first few months in the army, Viktor vowed to himself that he would not make trouble. But by Christmas, what with malnutrition and cold, his control was wearing thin. One day a sergeant took exception to the way he completed the morning run, and sent him to clean the latrines. Viktor bowed his head and trudged away. There was a song that he used to repeat to calm himself down, about a happy, drunk, naked woman in a supermarket, but this time it did not diffuse his anger. As he bent over the first pan and began to scrub, two second-year men came in and saw him.

'Look at the little shit-lover,' one jeered. 'Like getting your hands dirty, do you?'

Viktor said nothing.

'Let's help him out, lads,' said the other, standing over him and undoing his flies. 'We'll wash your hands for you.'

Before he had realised what he was doing, Viktor was shaking his senior until the latter's eyes popped.

'What's all this?' the sergeant bellowed, entering.

The second-year men were sent away, Viktor returned to his scrubbing and the rest of the day passed without incident – until the evening, when they came to pay Viktor a visit, along with a few of their friends. They pinned him in the corner and broke his jaw.

For two weeks, he wore a metal brace, while his commanding officer tried to extract names from him. Since perestroika they couldn't ignore these things completely. But Viktor, looking him straight in the eye, muttered only that he'd slipped in the shower and, sir, it was painful to talk.

'My God,' exclaimed the CO after a second interview, exasperated, 'The number of injuries these men sustain in the shower room. It's a wonder we allow them to wash at all.'

As Viktor lay there recovering, the guys came to see him again. 'Here,' one said, 'we heard you kept your mouth shut.'

'Not that he had much choice,' sniggered the other.

'We brought you something to make the time pass.' They produced a jam jar containing spirit, the sort that was kept in the tank shed to clean parts. 'Drink it down. It'll do you good.'

Viktor opened his mouth as far as he was able – about an inch – and sucked the spirit through his teeth. Halfway through he stopped, retching, but they tipped the jar up and sent a great gulp flooding down his throat and chin. When it was finished, they gave him water and clouted him on the shoulder. 'See you,' they said, and left.

'After that it was all right,' Viktor continued, topping up his glass. 'Normal. And, you know, when I got into second year, I did the same. We all did.'

It is a commonplace among Russian mothers that their sons are changed for the worse by their military service. He left such a good boy, they lament. Never been away from

home, seventeen, mild as milk. The army ruined him. Now he
drinks, and when he's drunk he gets angry, and as for his
feet! The smell of them! Nonsense, reply the fathers. I came
through it all right, didn't I? They have to learn to be men.
You learn a lot in the army, oh, it's amazing how fast you
learn . . .

I didn't see much of Ashot apart from that one afternoon. He
changed money for us, drooping his eyelids as he counted out
the notes; occasionally he sold on some cannabis, measured by
the glass, although he can't have made much money from the
deals. None of our Armenians conformed to the stereotype –
grasping, wily, flash with their money. They were as shabby as
the rest of us, but something kept them separate. He and the
other Armenians – Garo, round and jolly, with a bristly face
like a pirate's, Pasha, and the *Komendant* – sat together night
after night behind a closed door, and all we heard of them was
the buzz of conversation and laughter that seeped out into the
corridor. I asked Mitya about it.

'It's very simple.' He shrugged, slightly exasperated. 'The
historical imperative for them to hate Russians has been
supplemented by personal experience.' After a pause he
added, 'Military service is just one example. Men are sent
thousands of miles to regiments made up of the multitude of
friendly Soviet peoples. It's meant to turn them all into
Soviet patriots. After two years of the army, you can
imagine, they go home hating each other even more than
they did in the first place –'

This was the map of the Soviet Union that the boys picked up: Armenians hated Azeris, Chechens hated Ossetians, ethnic minorities hated Russians, Russians hated Jews, and everyone hated the lads from Moscow – so pleased with themselves, looking down their noses, with that nasal accent that made you grit your teeth. They were sent food parcels with condensed milk and jellies and little hunters' sausages, the kind of delicacies you could only get on Kalininsky Prospect. They paid for it though. The men made sure those Muscovite noses paid for it.

The point was, Mitya explained, you had to watch out for the Caucasians and the Central Asians. The guys who beat you up and bullied you weren't out to kill you, although it did happen – games that went too far, people who didn't know how to take a beating. You still had to be careful, but that was to be expected. The dangerous ones, though, were the wild boys from the mountains and the desert who instantly established a clan system within the camp and who'd grown up knowing how to fight. They carried knives with blades as supple as grass, that twanged in their hands if you passed them too close in the corridor. 'All right, calm yourself,' you'd say, not knowing if they felt their honour had been compromised, if they even understood you. They were different. It was just one of the things you had to accept in the army.

'When I see the news,' Mitya said, 'I always wonder if I'll see one of the boys I knew, up there in the mountains. They're fighting now, I'm sure of it. They had a worse time than us in the army, of course. If they survived that . . . And if the army taught them one thing, it was to stick together.'

On the first day of spring, Mitya and I walked down to the reservoir, past trees almost bare of snow. The ice still held and several fishermen were sitting by their iceholes for another day's cold, silent vigil. These were the fanatics. The fish they caught were not at all good to eat; in fact most were poisoned by the dirty water. Occasionally fishermen tried to sell them by the roadside, slapping a couple of pike on a plastic bag laid down in the mud. They did not look tempting. And to go out on the lake now, so late in the season . . . Apparently these men knew special paths, recognised the thin patches by sight and calculated to the hour when the ice would finally splinter. All the same, every year there were casualties.

There was a soft breeze, and for the first time in months I was outside without hat, gloves and scarf; the air on my forehead and cheeks felt wonderfully free, and at last I could move without slipping and watching my feet. Mitya and I ran until we came to a stop, puffing, and sat on a railing by the water.

'Remember the yacht we were going to live on?' Mitya said. 'Let's sail it through the Black Sea in the summer. The Crimean coast, past Odessa, Yalta, and to Batumi . . . It's a pity we'll have to avoid Abkhazia.'

'Perhaps you could come and visit me in England this summer?'

Mitya looked at me and smiled. 'If you'd like me to.'

When it grew cold, we turned back to the hostel, stopping to buy snowdrops from a babushka standing by the bridge.

'The spring arrives with them, children. Have two bunches,' she implored. 'The wind's chilly, I'll go home if you take them.'

I was sniffing the icy petals as we came up the stairs and heard it: a high, long howl that grew in volume, choked, and continued. Someone shouted with it and silenced it. Instantly it began again. It made my heart thump. By the time we got to the fourth floor, there was a crowd outside the Armenians' room.

The *Komendant* came out and pushed past us. 'Get out of the way.'

'But what is it? Is someone hurt?'

'Ashot,' said Garo, appearing in the doorway. His round face was slack and pale. 'The Azeris have shelled his village in Karabakh. Half the houses are hit. His brother is dead and God knows who else.'

Within the room Ashot stopped howling and began to knock his head slowly and deliberately against the wall.

'Those bastards,' Garo said. 'We'll kill them.'

The reservoir held for a few more days. The following week I saw a couple of fishermen heading out across it, intent on a last catch, but by the end of the month great cracks had appeared; the water was bubbling and hissing through them, tearing the ice apart. From the centre of the bridge Mitya and

I watched slabs like tectonic plates start to move. Footprints could still be seen on some of them, and bits of debris from the life they had supported: sticks, broken baskets, a single shoe. The sheets of ice drifted beneath us, gathering speed as they made their way towards the sea.

· 17 ·

Iron Boots

If you're a mushroom, you must jump in the basket.

Russian proverb

Spring arrived with the frenzy of the habitually late. One morning the air was balmy and buds appeared on the trees; two days later the whole town was bursting out in foliage and the inhabitants of Voronezh strolled about in flowery dresses, short sleeves and sandals. They seemed to have wiped the memory of winter from their minds; their serene expressions congratulated each other on their good fortune – no, their foresight – in choosing to live in a place with such a pleasant climate, a climate in which cucumbers and tomatoes grew with such juicy vigour.

The whole city all of a sudden had become *dachniki*, country dwellers with mud under their fingernails, who endured the week in the city only to hurry to the bus station and head for the country every Friday. They crammed into their Ladas, onto trolley buses and *elektrichki*, some travelling as far as a couple of hundred kilometres to open up their little wooden dachas and sow their seeds into the black earth.

In the evenings out there the men built a fire for the *shash-lyk* and fussed around it like surgeons, issuing peremptory orders: 'Bring the meat out! And a plate, please! Quick, vodka, we need vodka here now!' Every Russian man is, of course, an expert at the barbecue. When the meat is finally ready, they sit around the fire and eat it with flat Georgian bread and a handful of herbs; later on, someone pulls out a guitar and starts singing. The nostalgia for what is described as 'nature', a yearning which hangs over the bumpy, open-ended roads of their cities and in the concrete stairwells of their tower blocks, is here at its most acute. The succulent greenery that emits little rustles and creaks as it sprouts gives off an irresistible whiff of expectancy.

In the bus station, an English boy called John and I joined the crowd of *dachniki* heading in the direction of Kursk. It was five in the morning and we were going to the wedding of a couple I didn't know. Well, I'd met Slava, the groom, a friend of Emily's who burst into tears in our room back in September and begged her to help him with a visa. He was going to visit his girlfriend Lucy in Manchester. Emily did what she could to help, and so when their wedding was organised Slava reappeared with her invitation. But Emily was away, and such is my shameless passion for weddings that when Slava asked me instead, I couldn't help accepting.

'It will be nice for Lucy to have an English companion, as

her family can't come,' said Slava, hastily improvising a reason for my attendance. When the occasion demands it, Russians are the most polite people in the world. 'You can come with John, he's going to be our witness.'

The bus to Kursk took five hours: five hours of flat, unhedged farmland, and all the way John, who knew Lucy from Manchester, sat beside me sighing and plucking nervously at his beard. The male witness at a wedding has various duties apart from signing the register. He must look after the bride and groom, make sure their glasses are constantly filled, and propose a whole series of toasts, the longer and more poetic the better. He is also the defender of the bride's honour for the day. At a certain moment it is customary for a group of marauding guests to swoop down and steal away the bride from her husband, and then it is the witness's duty to capture her back. Sometimes this is done by paying a ransom in hard cash, but more often a feat is required of him. The bride's white satin stiletto is produced and filled with vodka, and the witness must drink it down. Depending on the size of the bride's foot, it can contain most of a bottle . . . Then, ideally, the witness bursts into the place where the bride is held, tosses her over his shoulder in a fireman's lift and deposits her back at her husband's side with roar of triumph.

'You don't know Lucy,' John said gloomily. 'She's not big, but – well, she's not tiny.'

That was still not the worst of it. The most important duty of all, the one that the male witness is never allowed to shirk, is to kiss the female witness. After a reasonable time complimenting her on her turquoise outfit – a quarter of an hour will do – tradition demands that he drag her into a bedroom and grapple her on the bed where the guests have left their coats. And if he doesn't, make no mistake, she'll drag him. At this stage John hadn't made any public announcements about his sexuality, but it was clear that the idea of the female witness filled him with foreboding.

Now and then the bus stopped to let a couple of *dachniki* out. They shouldered their bags and trudged away, and I was reminded of a proverb quoted by Pasternak: 'Life is not as easy as crossing a field.' The black earth, freshly sliced and turned, was so rich that it seemed you could spoon it straight into your mouth. As the sun climbed, the wet soil began to steam and the bus was filled with its smell. When the Nazis invaded the Ukraine, they were so astonished by the black earth that they looted it. A whole convoy of lorries was loaded up and sent back to Germany; even now there must be German farmers, who, every springtime, lift their heads and sniff this same, delicious scent, as sweet and dark as chocolate pudding.

In Kursk, one of Slava's relatives, Anatoly, was waiting for us at the station. He was a huge man. His neck was corded with tendons, his chest bulged, and his face was full of guileless, rapacious delight.

'Welcome!' he bellowed, thumping John on the back. 'Guests! You've come far –'

'Well, only from Voronezh,' said John. He looked more nervous than ever.

'Far!' insisted Anatoly. 'We must celebrate. Immediately.'

We bounced along the wide roads of Kursk in his car, a squashy Pobeda – Victory – to an apartment on the outskirts of town.

'Welcome, dear guests,' beamed Slava's father and mother, shepherding us into the kitchen. 'You'll be hungry after your journey. Sit down, please! Anatoly, will you –?'

Anatoly nodded and took up a glass. 'Dear friends, we are glad to welcome you into our home. There will be many toasts today, and each one will be longer than the last, so the first one had better be short. To our meeting!'

So we tossed back a shot of vodka, which, at eleven in the morning, on a five o'clock start, an empty stomach and a long bus ride, had an explosive effect. The order had gone out: take no prisoners. The festivities were beginning.

In the summer of 1943, the plains around Kursk were the site of the greatest tank battle in history. Manstein threw whole panzer armies into a desperate attempt to destroy Russian armour, and so to stave off what he already knew was an inevitable defeat. The plan, having claimed thousands of lives, failed. After the war the city was rebuilt around a series of huge memorials that are still at the centre of every ritual event, and weddings in particular. After the registry office service, Lucy and Slava were driven to each one of them in a taxi decorated with Russian and British flags. Under the solemn gaze of the video camera, the bride and groom crossed expanses of concrete paving and laid carnations before the lists of the dead. This was the first part of the ceremony.

Back in the apartment, Slava's parents were waiting to greet their son and daughter-in-law with bread and salt. A horseshoe-shaped table had been set up in the sitting room and loaded with dishes of *zakuski*, salads, meats, smoked fish and every conceivable Russian delicacy. Uncles and aunts were standing in the hall, each ruddier, jollier and stouter than their neighbour.

'Oh, what a beauty,' they cried, kissing Lucy and pinching her cheek. 'Now come along, come along.'

And they hurried into the sitting room to take their places and boss each other around some more. Slava's mother, carrying in still more plates of food, nodded at Slava and Lucy.

'Sit down, you two.'

They sat at the top of the horseshoe, holding hands and looking shyly around them.

'Now, Anatoly, please!' called out the jolliest of all the uncles, raising his glass.

'Spring has come, the trees are in leaf after our long winter,' Anatoly started, and the aunts settled down contentedly, recognising the beginning of a good long toast when they heard one. 'The most fortunate time of year for a wedding . . .' My mind drifted; I tried to imagine this scene taking place in Mitya's parents' flat, and failed. Finally a change of tone from Anatoly signalled a conclusion. 'May your life together be full of light, health and joy.'

We drank to that and began on the *zakuski*. This was the

second part of the ceremony. More toasts followed in quick succession, the guests outdoing one another in eloquence, the plates of *zakuski* emptied and were immediately replaced by even larger, fuller plates, and as the hours passed, the ritual repetition of good wishes gave the proceedings a faintly hypnotic air. Every now and then, the cry of *gorko!* – bitter! – went up, which is the signal for the bride and groom to kiss. Slava and Lucy blushingly complied, while the most ribald of the uncles timed them on his stopwatch. And whenever there was a lull in the proceedings, the female witness, a determined blonde called Ina, fulfilled John's worst expectations by suggesting a toast '*na brudershaft*', with linked arms.

'Oh, Ina!' everyone exclaimed, in the indulgent tone that meant *she is a one*. We looked on as they drained their champagne glasses. John, laughing nervously, attempted to hold her away from him by bracing his arm, but she seized him by the beard and kissed him all the same.

'What a handsome man,' said the elderly aunt sitting next to me. 'If I was Ina's age, I wouldn't let him get away.' She roared with laughter. 'There were no men when I was her age, you see. After the war there were seven women to one man, lucky boys –'

'Did you ever marry?'

'Oh yes, I married just before the war. Vladimir was his name, poor man, Vladimir Aleksandrovich. He was killed at Smolensk. He hadn't had much of a life . . . Still, I shouldn't talk about that here. Thank God those days are over.'

It was evening by this time; we'd been at the table for five hours at least, and Slava and Lucy were looking pale and overwhelmed. I sympathised; an age seemed to have passed since the morning. But the older generation showed no signs of slowing up.

'Come on, Charlotte!' the aunts suddenly announced. 'Come with us! You know how to dance to this modern music.'

Someone put on a tape of Showaddywaddy and we danced in the hall – me in the middle surrounded by middle-aged ladies. After a time we worked out a little routine which made them laugh so much that they had to hold onto their bosoms.

'Don't stop!' one of them gasped. 'I'm just getting started.'

They quietened down a little after three in the morning, but when John and I left to catch the bus back to Voronezh, they were beginning again, as spruce and rosy-cheeked as ever. They had stamina, that generation, and they approached an event such as this one with determination, not with our lightweight, stay-as-long-as-we-feel-like-it attitude. Each wedding party is a victory celebration, in a way, and a reiteration of Kursk's heroic survival in 1943. Each marriage is a triumph of spring, of immortality. It demands time and application.

Early in May, Mitya and I walked past the shop called Sport and saw shiny, fold-up bicycles being unpacked. Despite the fact that there was a constant shortage of bicycles and these were the first in the shop for months, central planning had decreed that they should be sold for about fifty cents, or the price of a pot of honey. So I became the owner of a bright green bicycle. And when Mitya took his bike down from its place strapped to the ceiling of his parents' hall, we started making our own pilgrimages to the countryside.

On Victory Day, a week or so after the wedding of Slava and Lucy, we pedalled out of town with a picnic in a rucksack. The streets were cleared of cars, and bunting was fluttering all the way along Revolution Prospect. Stalls selling vodka and buns had been set up at regular intervals along the pavement. Families were strolling down the centre of the Prospect hand in hand, wearing their best clothes; their little daughters had ribbons at both ends of their plaits. It was still early, but against the walls, the drunks were already lurching at one another and discussing impossible things. Later on we were going to a jazz concert and other festivities, but just for the afternoon, we were heading for the woods. It was a glittering, cloudless day and even in the centre of town the smell of the forest could occasionally be detected, a sharp and bosky scent that drew us through the suburbs and along the river to the birch trees.

Our *shashlyk* were a makeshift affair. There'd been no time to marinade the meat, so we bought a small chicken and skewered it, whole, on a stick. The fire is meant to be carefully fostered in a metal drum of some kind, which we didn't have; also the wood was wet. But Mitya remembered a can of lighter fluid in his bag which produced a leap of flame and foul-smelling black smoke. The chicken, drumsticks outstretched like a martyr, charred slowly in the fumes.

'Now let's have a drink,' said Mitya, producing a bottle of vodka.

'I thought you said you were going to buy beer.'

'There was only the expensive beer. Anyway, vodka's better. It's a holiday today.'

'But we talked about it. We said we weren't going to drink vodka today, or not until this evening, anyway.'

'Come on, we're in the woods! It's so beautiful! Don't spoil it.' Mitya handed me a glass of vodka. 'The first toast is to us. Let's drink to all our future picnics. To English picnics this summer, maybe.'

I drank the vodka. The less I felt like drinking spirits, the more Mitya insisted on his daily intake. It had got to the stage where he regularly drank so much that the next day he remembered nothing after nine in the evening: sitting in the hostel until one in the morning, walking home and going to bed were all expunged. Out there among the birch trees, I didn't see the point of having a fight with him about it: our afternoon would only be ruined. But by the time I was back in Britain and trying to make sense of what had happened, it was moments like these that struck me as fatal.

'Don't worry,' said Mitya. 'You worry too much. It's fine. Listen – I heard this Chinese fairy story on the radio, it's so good.' He lit a cigarette. 'There was a man who lived in the mountains and when he was very young, he put on a pair of iron boots. And he never took them off. He wore them to walk all the way down to the river to collect water and to carry the water back up to his hut. He wore them to till his fields, he wore them to drive his animals to pasture and back again, he even wore them in bed. For twenty years he lived like this, until suddenly he took them off.'

'And then?'

Mitya blew smoke into the air and grinned. 'He flew away! He took his iron boots off and just flew up into the air. Don't you think the meat is cooked by now?'

Against all the odds, the chicken was delicious; we ate it with bread and tomatoes – the first fresh tomatoes I'd tasted for months – and I couldn't help feeling happy.

In the late afternoon we biked back through the woods and parted when we arrived at the Central Market, me to go back to the hostel, Mitya to go home.

'Meet you at seven outside the concert hall, all right?'

'OK. Don't drink too much tonight, though, will you? You turn into someone I don't know.'

He laughed. 'Listen to her! You sound like a Russian woman. I won't, I promise. Just enough.'

At quarter past seven, there was no sign of Mitya. People were streaming in to hear the jazz; they had dressed up and were chatting eagerly as they went in. Fifteen minutes more passed, and finally a figure appeared running across Lenin Square.

'Sorry,' he panted when he got to me. His eyes had the red-rimmed, blank look that meant he'd had at least a bottle. 'Lapochka and I . . . we got held up.'

Lapochka, Petya Pravda and a girl I didn't know were

walking behind, gesticulating energetically to each other in the way that very drunk people do.

'After you went back to the hostel, Lapochka and I met up for a bit of a celebration,' Mitya explained. 'We just came to get you. The concert doesn't start till seven forty-five. Come on –'

We went to the back of the Opera building to a dingy yard. Four blokes were already there, sharing a couple of bottles of vodka.

'Look,' Mitya pointed at them. 'It's Victory Day. It would be disloyal not to get drunk.'

The others arrived and produced some brandy. 'No glasses. It's straight from the neck.'

We stood in this filthy yard, where a stray dog was picking about on a mound of rubbish, and drank the bottle. After a time my fury abated and instead tears rose to the backs of my eyes. Mitya put his arms around me.

'Don't worry, *milaya*,' he said, 'We're just taking our iron boots off, don't you see?'

'Taking them off and . . . flying away!' Petya Pravda repeated, giggling.

We saw only part of the concert. Our arrival caused a small commotion; we had seats right at the front and the audience were united in their disgust at this shambling group who were arriving late and clearly the worse for wear.

'It's a disgrace!' hissed the usherette, as she led us to our row.

It didn't help when Lapochka pointed out a remarkable similarity between the musicians' appearances and their instruments. The tuba player was shiny and tubular; the pianist was straight-backed with black and white teeth. The boys were convulsed with laughter, and the people behind began to whisper furiously. After a while, Petya Pravda leaned across with a confidential air and said, 'I don't know about you, but I'm thirsty.'

'We need a beer to set us right. Let's go.'

It was dark outside. I sat on a bench while they bought beer from the kiosks outside the Spartacus cinema. Most of the women seemed to have gone home but there were still crowds of men milling about in the streets, drinking and spitting onto the pavement. Under the yellowish streetlights their faces were shiny and, it seemed to me, hostile. Music was blaring out from the kiosks.

'You bastard, that's mine!' shouted someone from the park behind us. 'Give it!'

I turned around. Through the darkness I could just make out two figures struggling on the grass. Men were standing around and watching them fight.

Mitya and Lapochka were laughing, looking over towards the classical facade of the cinema.

'Where's Petya gone?'

'Over there,' said Lapochka. 'He wants to climb up to Spartacus.'

'Let's watch,' shouted Mitya. 'Come on!'

It happened fast after that. Mitya and Lapochka staggered across the park and headed across the road to the cinema. As they reached the pavement a police van drew up and two policemen jumped out and slid open the doors.

'Right, boys,' I heard them say, 'To the *vytrezvitel* with you.'
By the time I caught up, Mitya and Lapochka were in the van
and the doors were closed.

'Where are you taking them?'

'To the lockup to sleep it off. They'll be out in the morning.
Go home, *dyevushka*. Your friends are bad news.'

In the silence that the van left behind it, I sensed myself
being noticed. A woman walking alone at this time of night
could only be working. I began to thread my way through the
crowd in the direction of the hostel.

'Hey, *dyevka*, you on your own?' asked a guy, putting his
hand on my elbow.

'No,' I snapped and shook him off. He was too drunk to
respond. On Revolution Prospect there was a fight going on
outside one of the bars; I crossed over and a group of men
gestured to me.

'You coming to join us, beauty?'

I walked on. The trolleybus stops were empty, which could
only mean that the trolley buses had stopped running for the
night. I stuck my thumb out for a taxi and almost immediately
a car stopped beside me.

'Where to?' said the driver.

'Just up Friedrich Engels Street.'

He nodded, and it was only when I was already sitting
down that I saw there was another man in the back.

'How about a drink? Have a little one with us.' The man
lurched across and put an arm around me.

'No, thank you,' I replied coldly.

'Oh. Cigarette, then?'

'I don't drink or smoke. I'm a Baptist,' I added. 'From Riga.'

'Oh.' He drew away. As I'd hoped, the bit about Riga stopped them asking me about my accent. At the hostel they let me out politely. My pulse was still racing when I got back to our room.

There, in my bed, lay Mitya. He was fully dressed, asleep and snoring. Over the other side of the room, Emily sat up and looked at me.

'You're back. I was worrying.'

'When did he get here?'

'Oh, ten minutes ago. I couldn't get a word out of him. But someone said he was taken to the *vytrezvitel* in a van, then let out straight away. They didn't keep him – I suppose tonight they didn't have room.'

A shiny purple bruise was appearing on his temple. It was quiet; Ira was sleeping in the third bed, breathing softly.

'We have to ring and confirm our return tickets this week,' Emily whispered.

In two months we were going home. I squeezed into the bed beside Mitya, blinked at the ceiling and thought: flying away. Relief, like sleep, engulfed me.

Peter Truth

There's no returning to the heart:
The dead to the environs go
Away from resurrected stone.

Reducible to soil and snow
They hem the town in hard as bone:
The outer zones of Voronezh.

Alan Sillitoe, *Love in the
Environs of Voronezh*, 1968

Petya Pravda's dead. At the end of spring he died, as elongated and translucent as an icon. His mother found him in the morning and straight away set up a wail that brought in the neighbours: Pyotr! Petya! My little Petya! And they hurried in, old Kolya hitching up his belly, stinking of hangover, Anna Nikolaevna already back from the market, and Petya's aunt Ludmilla, wrapped in her dressing gown with emerald eyeshadow on one eye.

It wasn't the first time they'd come running to this cry. More than once, Kolya had dashed off for the doctor, while

Ludmilla tremblingly applied the first aid she learnt at the factory. Petya suddenly blinked, so pale it seemed the colour had left even his irises, with a ghastly crimson ring of Ludmilla's lipstick smeared around his mouth. All the women started laughing and crying. Ludmilla wiped the lipstick off with a thumb. And Petya just lay there and, after a few moments, turned on his side and closed his eyes.

This time, however, he stopped breathing during the night, and by morning there was nothing they could do. His mother, who was almost crippled by arthritis, was persuaded to rest. Kolya closed Petya's eyes with fifty-kopeck pieces, and the women organised the funeral. By the time we saw him he was stretched out on the table and surrounded by crosses and incense. I thought how amused he would have been to be given an Orthodox sendoff – yet, in a way, it wasn't inappropriate.

Pyotr Pravda – Peter Truth. Part of the burden of life that Petya found repellent must have been his name – how to live up to such a name! The first Pyotr Pravda, his grandfather, a railway worker who fought in the civil war, had taken the surname as a new beginning in a brand-new world. There was a black-and-white photograph of him in their front room: a bony face with dark eyes, a medal-decked chest and the Soviet passport, touched up with red ink, poking out of his top pocket. Petya looked identical, although he had none of the pride that bristles from his grandfather's portrait. His mother got him to hang it up not so long ago. 'There,' she said. 'I only knew him when he came back from the camps, like a little old nut and grumpy as hell. May he rest in peace,' she added.

His grandfather's truth had aged by the time Petya inherited it. Not that it bothered him either way at first, of course. The fat little Petya of early photographs, wrapped up in six layers of artificial fur so he stood stiff as an overstuffed bear, holding the string of a toboggan and beaming as hard as his chubby, chilly face would allow – he was no child philosopher. Perhaps the shadow that crept over him was particular to his experience – vodka in the courtyard at fifteen, military service and beatings by the tough guys, a two-room flat with an invalid mother and Friday evenings in small-town Russia, a pack of young boys bursting with energy and nowhere, nowhere for them to expend it. By the early nineties, the truth was a sensation-seeking little rag. No kind of word to have on your identity card.

At the beginning of the year Petya was at university with the rest of us. He was too thin, with a boyish, energetic manner, and he wore the same threadbare jacket summer and winter. He was not a diligent student; he and the Narcomen kept themselves amused without having to attend lectures. The exams, when the time came, were oral – no problem. I sat in on an exam of Petya's, once. Mitya and I had been up all night with him and Lapochka when he decided that I must go with him as his talisman. It was the kind of joke he enjoyed.

Petya's mother had a tendency to keep every bit of paper,

including the doctor's notes from the days when her illness was not so advanced. So the next day we arrived at the faculty together and presented the lecturer with a note stating that P. Pravda had arthritic cramps, and three days' bed rest was essential.

The professor, Maria Mikhailovna, was a motherly figure well known for her susceptibility to young men, but even she raised her eyebrows a little as Petya assured her that he wouldn't have missed this exam for the world: 'To lose a chance to defend my Pushkin would set me back even further, Maria Mikhailovna. You understand me.' He fixed her with his dark eyes. 'But Charlotte has agreed to rub the area during the exam, if you don't object.' And I stood behind him with my hands poised ready on his shoulders.

'Pushkin massages his words into place,' Petya began, making me snort. He continued smoothly. 'Even the clumsiest, most unmanageable Russian verb, stiff with prefixes and trailing an endless, glutinous reflexive agreement, is made to feel supple and extraordinarily powerful . . . because each of them occupies an unassailable position in Pushkin's world, in the world of language, a world that is lucid and vivid, ordered and yet more spontaneous than our own – a world that, in fact, is more real than reality.'

Maria Mikhailovna smiled dreamily and marked him 'excellent'.

The Narcomen rolled their joints on the photograph of old Pyotr Pravda and talked about their latest discoveries in music or literature. Yet they shared the conviction that brains were no good to them in their Russia. 'What's the point?' they said to me. 'To be successful, you either need connections, or you need to be a thug. You don't need brains.'

This made me angry. 'But how can you say so? Maybe under Brezhnev it was true, but now there is every opportunity! You can work, write, start a business, be free . . .'

'Oh yes?' The Horse glanced at me coolly. 'For a moment drop your assumption that elections and a free press mean democracy, which is the solution to all social ills, and look. Free thought? I've had that all my life. Of course there was a shortage of books and tapes before, but we passed them around . . . we got hold of things. We had less, but we appreciated it more. Travel? It was in the old days that we could travel, spend the summer in Dubrovnik, sail on Lake Baikal, walk in Karelia. A ticket to Moscow cost 7 roubles then – now it's 25,000. I couldn't afford to go up to Moscow, let alone look for a job there, rent a flat for hundreds of dollars a month, buy a suit . . . Start a business? Just look at the kind of guys running businesses down here in Voronezh. Do you think it is a coincidence that they share the low and bulging brow, the arms too long for their bodies, the form of apes in their maroon jackets? The only businesses that succeed in this transitional period are rackets. And I'm not interested.'

'It's not just that you don't need brains,' Lapochka added. 'It's a disadvantage to have them. Look at the intelligent Russians: either they have left the country or they are starving.'

I felt chastened.

Soon after, Petya was deemed unsuitable to remain a university student. Professors other than Maria Mikhailovna showed signs of restlessness when Petya defended his exams. They wanted a display of linguistic developments pioneered by Pushkin, a knowledge of the social background that gave rise to Pushkin's verse. The rest of the country might be going to pot, but within the concrete confines of the university, the old standards still prevailed. Students still took their classes in ideological enlightenment; the boys spent Mondays wriggling across patches of rough grass in camouflage while the girls learnt to assemble a Kalashnikov in fifteen seconds and administered first aid to mannequins of the Red Army. The collapse of the Soviet Union did not alter the truth behind Brezhnev's ideology: Russia is great. Russia is powerful. To her greatness and her power every citizen must pay his homage and make his sacrifice, as our parents and grandparents did. Why, otherwise, did all the Soviet martyrs have to die? Anyway – look at this boy. He's quite plainly a degenerate.

Petya sat before them with a fixed smile, and attempted to interest them in Buddhism. Nirvana, he suggested, was a civilised type of afterlife, a Communist type, even. Then he went out and got drunk, and had a fight with the doorman at the university buffet. He wasn't taken to court but it was the end of his student days.

His mother wept and took it up with the bureaucrats, but it soon turned out she needed more that her invalid's pension to get the decision overturned. So instead she exchanged her father's medals for a wad of greasy roubles, counted out by an old friend of hers – an engineer now turned taxi driver and antique dealer – and booked Petya an appointment for an alcohol cure.

'Hmmm, been having a few too many, have you?' said the doctor cheerily. 'Your Mama's paid me in advance for the pleasure of fitting you with a capsule. You know how it works, don't you? A classy little container of poison under the skin of your arm. It sits there all snug and not causing you a moment's trouble, until you have a few grammes of alcohol. Partial dissolution of the casing follows, and *yolki palki!* you feel sick as a rabbit. Outcome: you stay off the stuff. How do you like the sound of that? You've got to be careful though, you can do yourself an injury if you go on a real binge.'

Petya sat on a chair looking faintly green. His head was pounding. He was desperate for a drink. 'Listen, doctor.' He raised his eyes. 'This is going to do me no good. My system won't take it. What do you say to splitting the cash and you get to keep the capsule?'

The doctor studied him for a minute, then measured his blood pressure. He checked Petya's reflexes and shone a light in his ears. 'Well . . .' he said at last. 'Sixty–forty, and you're on.'

Petya slept a lot that winter, grew thinner and older. Once or twice Mitya and I stood outside his window and called 'Petyuk!' in a whisper and he appeared in his dressing gown.

He sat down with us outside and lit up a ready-rolled joint, his eyes huge, almond-shaped and expressionless.

How is a man to live? In the old style, this was our subject as we sat in the yard under the gaze of his black eyes. And as the post-Soviet world grew increasingly grotesque, Petya decided that the only sincere way of life was in the mind. He became a zealot. 'From henceforth I have decided to live by the seasons,' he announced to us all. 'In the summer – alcohol. In autumn, the new harvest of grass. In the winter, fireworks and speed. And in the spring, all damp and tender – the only thing for it is opium.'

'Petya is a dualist, you understand,' Lapochka said. 'He sees that freedom lies in the spirit, not the body. Demands of the world – to earn a living, to get a degree, to covet and desire and envy, there's no difference between them! – they are all temptations that distract one from matters of the spirit. It's not Petya that's irresponsible. Quite the opposite – the irresponsible ones are those that devote their lives to their career and their family, at the expense of their soul.'

Petya saw my face and laughed. 'Don't listen to this anti-social nonsense!' he said, and changed the subject. I never discovered if Lapochka was expressing Petya's ideas, or his own.

Alcohol, of course, was always available. But it didn't satisfy Petya. 'In reality,' he used to say, 'I do not like these official intoxicants. They make you stupid and lustful.'

Autumn was a pleasant season. Cannabis was for sale all

over the place, if Lapochka's neighbours were out. But when the winter set in, with month after month of dark, cold days, Petya needed to go faster and further. Then he'd try the university research laboratories for amphetamines – he had an acquaintance there, a panda-eyed girl who'd help him out. It wasn't such a smooth journey, though. A couple of times her supplies gave Petya's mother a scare.

Finally, the thaw came, and with it heroin from Central Asia. In April, a group of us went out to a dacha one weekend. The breeze was exhilarating, life was stirring in the woods. The others hurried on, leaving Mitya and me to gaze at the birds wheeling above the trees. By the time we arrived they were all lying on the sofa and smiling beatifically, apart from Petya, who stood and looked them over.

'All of this free market, it is just as stupid as our Soviet materialism . . .' he began. 'Now the people think that they were wrong all those years to believe in Communism, because it never gave them the glossy washing machines and American trainers that the free market has . . . But they don't understand . . . Any philosophy which has as its highest aim a state in which everyone has washing machines, whether it achieves that by collective efforts or individual, is poor and mean. Do you see?'

'And what about your mother?' I meant that she needed him.

'My mother – she suffocates me with her preventative medicines, with her meals, her Eat up!, her obsession with the flesh when she is almost a cripple, she should recognise that it is not important . . . Everywhere it is the same. In the street shops, posters, people shoving each other to get the last tin of pork, beggars – why don't they just die? They'd be happier. Even in the church it's all money, money, gold icons, fat priests, and people hoping their loathsome flesh will be preserved for all eternity . . . it's all disgusting.' He grinned at us. 'If only I were a religious man, how people would admire me.'

The Voronezh police didn't think much of Petya's theories. In fairness to them, they didn't think much at all. They arrested him one drunken evening and took him to the lockup, where they advised him that such a carry-on was bad for his health. To push the point home they broke a couple of his ribs and gave his kidneys a good bruising. His mother blanched and put him to bed, but he couldn't settle until he'd downed the Lily-of-the-Valley cologne he'd given her for International Women's Day.

The ribs healed, leaving Petya breathless but apparently stronger than ever. He wore the same thin little jacket and trousers, out of which his bony, bruised arms and feet protruded; his skin turned waxy. He moved with jerky, horrible energy and he was always making plans. After Victory Day, when he tried to crown Spartacus with laurels, he disappeared for several days. Then he suddenly rang Lapochka at five in the morning and said, 'Let's go to Central Asia. In the summer. We'll study the way of the dervishes.'

His aunt Ludmilla said, 'He's not long for us.'

With the warmer weather, according to the Horse, came an especially pure load of heroin. Petya had been warned, the Horse said, and Petya, more than anyone, knew the score. And the Horse shrugged.

The funeral was a pitiful affair. The photographs and paper rosettes that decorate Russian cemeteries give them a temporary, tattered look. The graves are inches apart; even in death Russians these days must be thrifty. Afterwards there was a wake back at the flat. We stood about feeling awkward until a few toasts were drunk – without clinking glasses, as is the custom when you drink to the dead. Slowly the atmosphere warmed up and the Narcomen, who had been looking forlorn, began to talk and gesticulate. Lapochka, while telling one of Petya's stories, knocked old Pyotr Pravda's photograph off the wall onto the samovar, breaking the glass, and his grimaces of apology made everyone laugh. We stayed till midnight, by which time the flat was a welter of plates, and tears, and jokes, and empty bottles.

Ludmilla kept an eye on Petya's mother for the next few weeks and made sure she ate. Even the Narcomen visited a couple of times. By Orthodox custom, however, the soul remains in this world for forty days before departing for ever to the next. So, forty days after his death, we met to say goodbye to Petya Pravda.

It was a less emotional event than the funeral. The Horse was leaving for St Petersburg the week after – he was having an exhibition. Petya's mother gave him paper and books that had been Petya's and a scolding to dress warmly.

I watched her bustle about the flat and wondered about her arthritis.

'Yes,' she said and for the first time that day her eyes filled with tears. 'It is strange, but the flat has become so warm since . . . since. It used to be damp, the draughts gave me so much pain, but you know, I am a crazy old woman, but I think it is my son looking after me.'

The photograph of old Pyotr Pravda was in its old place; without the glass, the resemblance to his grandson was even more marked. But after its steaming from the samovar, it was looking its age. The red of the passport had made a bloody wound down his chest. Around his head was a yellow–brown tea stain, and his dark eyes gazed out of this impromptu halo with a look of serene despair.

· 19 ·

Leaving

Let me go, return me, Voronezh:
you will drop or lose me,
you will let me fall or give me back.
Voronezh, you are a whim, Voronezh, you are a raven
and a knife.

Osip Mandelstam,
The Voronezh Notebooks, 1936

'Do you remember Smokey, Lapochka's friend?' Mitya asked.
'He's gone. He and a friend of his called Vlad went to the
Ukraine last week, and from there they're going to try and get
a boat to Bulgaria without a visa.'

'A summer holiday.' We were sitting on the Voronezh
beach – the sandbank at the edge of the reservoir – and eating
slabs of vanilla ice cream. It was so hot I was only half listening, wondering whether to move into the shade.

'Well, not exactly. From Bulgaria they think they can cross
into Yugoslavia and fight as mercenaries for the Serbs.'

'What? Do they have some idea about the unity of the
Slavs?'

'No.'

'Why then?'

'Why do you think? For the money.' Mitya was silent for a minute, then he added, 'And to get out of here, of course.'

Everyone seemed to be leaving. The Horse was going to paint in St Petersburg. Valya Uvarova was heading for the USA. Yuri, Emily's boyfriend, Igor and Lyuba all had places to study abroad. Sasha, the guy in the hostel who'd been in the Afghan war, had been wearing tinted glasses for the past six weeks. He'd had laser surgery to cure his short sight: it was one of the conditions of joining the French Foreign Legion.

'Seven years of service and then you get French citizenship,' he explained.

'Is it really worth it?'

'Of course it's worth it. In seven years I'll be thirty-one.' He grinned. 'If I make it.'

Even Lapochka was preparing to get out. He had scraped together ten dollars and an envelope containing articles from the *Voronezh Courier* that described him and the other Narcomen by name as degenerates. He was going to hitch to England with his ten dollars – he was sure he'd get there somehow – and demand asylum. The article proved that he was in danger in Voronezh from the growing influence of the 'red–brown coalition' – the old Communist and Nationalist parties whose bigotry brought them together. What were the odds that such a plan would succeed? But a year and a half later I met Lapochka bicycling down Upper Street in Islington as though he'd lived there all his life.

Our last weeks in Voronezh were astonishingly, gloriously hot. The pavements were dusty and ice-cream sellers stood in the shade of the knobbly plane trees with their cans shaped like milk churns, mopping their foreheads and uttering faint enticements.

'Creamy ices,' they murmured as you passed. 'Cool yourself . . . the healthiest, the purest.'

On the weekends the city emptied and even the weeks seemed to have a lackadaisical, gone-on-holiday slowness. Shop assistants propped open the doors and sat outside; they fanned themselves and almost forgot to terrorise their customers. Other strange phenomena occurred, which everyone ignored completely. One June morning I woke up to see the sun blazing in a turquoise sky and the air full of snowflakes.

'Oh,' Ira said, without even turning to see. 'It's *pukh*. When they planted all the poplar trees, they somehow got hold of the wrong sort, with seeds like this. So every June the Soviet Union is full of *pukh*. It gives people terrible asthma.'

The *pukh*, like cotton wool, settled in drifts, and small boys amused themselves by setting fire to it. Meanwhile on the corner of Friedrich Engels and Peace Prospect, a crater seven foot in diameter appeared overnight and was fenced off with a little piece of string. Since the thaw, roads had been caving in and flooding all over town wherever a pipe had burst. There were dozens of examples. On one occasion drivers waiting at a set of traffic lights suddenly found that their cars were standing in a foot of water. When they tried to drive away, their tyres seemed to have collapsed. They stepped out of their cars and screamed: the water was scalding hot. Their tyres had melted.

In the heat Emily and I began the task of packing up our lives. We staggered back and forth to the central post office, where an assistant wrapped our books in brown paper and sealed them with wax before sacrificing them to the Russian postal system. We took our bottles to the bottle bank and put the money into the fund for the farewell party, and then we sat for a long time smoking cigarettes and contemplating our room.

'You won't be able to take it all with you,' Sveta commented, before we'd even started. 'Anything you don't want –'

'Yes, Sveta, we know who to give it to.'

'All right, calm down.'

Sveta tactfully withdrew; or so we thought, until she reappeared ten minutes later with a couple of boxes.

'These are for whatever is left over,' she stated. 'Just put them all in there for me.' And she left again, quickly, having seen our expressions.

On the hottest day of all we took the *elektrichka* one last time and headed out into the woods for our leaving party. There was a crowd of us: almost all the English people, and the girls from Room 99, Yuri, Peanut, Yakov and Katya, Joe and Ira and all the rest. The train was full of city dwellers with the same idea, and the air was heavy with sweat. We barely squeezed into the doorway at the end of one carriage. The conversation turned to the matter of going abroad; we'd talked about nothing else for weeks.

'It's a two-year course,' said Yuri, who was going to England, 'and then maybe I'll stay there, who knows. If I can get a good job.'

'Don't you think you'd miss Russia?'

'Well, yes, but if I have the choice between sitting in Voronezh with no money and dreaming about going abroad, or sitting in England with five hundred dollars in my pocket and dreaming about Voronezh, I know which I'd take.'

'I can see exactly what you are going to become,' said Tanya. 'You'll come back to visit us and you'll be complaining, Oh, this country is so filthy, oh, why do they have this ridiculous system of queuing in shops!'

Yuri laughed. 'I'll come back and we'll have a huge party with as much of everything as we like.'

This was the first wave of purely economic emigration that Russia had seen; previously, exiles had always left with a certain glow of heroism, whether they were fleeing Tsarist censorship in the nineteenth century or persecution by the KGB in the twentieth. In Paris or New York they had dreamed and plotted revolution, so that at last they could go home. On the face of it, however, nothing would stop these young Russians from visiting their home whenever they wanted. But in practice Tanya was right. The invisible frontier that separates the West from the rest of the world would keep them apart. It would make it almost impossible for them to return, just as it was impossible for me to stay, for me to be any more Russian than I was.

When we reached the station, Mitya and I rode on ahead with most of the provisions. The path seemed perfectly clear: down to the river and along until we came upon the tents which Viktor had been setting up since morning. But somehow we found ourselves pushing our bicycles through a patch of thorny hillocks, lost. After a while the strap on my sandal snapped and I had to go barefoot; then Mitya had a puncture. When we finally arrived, the mood among the others was frosty. They'd been waiting for the food and drink for more than an hour.

'It's just typical of you two,' we were told. 'So selfish.'

As the sun fell over the river, the mosquitoes formed great dusty clouds above our camp. We lit a fire and tried to raise our spirits with alcohol. It was a perfect summer evening; golden light lay on the water until almost ten o'clock, and the clouds glowed pink above us. But the atmosphere did not improve. We sat huddled in the smoke, irritably slapping the insects away and failing to get the fire hot enough to cook the meat. By the time it was ready, the smell of roasting fat was enough to make my stomach turn. I crawled into a tent and lay there, shivering.

The next day, having wheeled our bicycles back to the station, Mitya and I sat on the grass and smoked. It was the middle of the day and I could barely open my eyes against the flat, white light. Mitya was also looking down, his face set in an expression that I recognised: very still, eyes narrowed.

When he spoke, it was distantly, as though I had already left.

'What will you do when you get back to England?'

'I don't know, see my family, get ready to go back to university. Miss you.' There was a pause. 'What will you do?'

'Oh, I'll . . . the same as ever. Work nights in the shop, go out to the woods, go to the cinema. Get drunk.'

'Who will you go to the cinema with?'

'I don't know.'

'I'm going to see how much a ticket will be for you to come over in August.'

Mitya sighed. 'Oh Charlotte, it's really not possible. I can't earn enough money before then, and I don't want to be paid for.'

'Don't be like that. You can pay me back later, whenever.'

'And how am I going to do that, I wonder? Shall I put it on my credit card, or shall I just rob a bank?'

There was a silence.

'It doesn't have to be the end,' I said. We'd been saying this to each other for weeks, trying to sound convincing.

'No, it doesn't,' muttered Mitya. 'I'm sorry.'

When the *elektrichka* finally arrived most of the window-panes in the carriage were missing, as usual, and the wind and engine noise made it impossible to talk. I watched Mitya as he lit another cigarette and smoked it out of the window. He was very pale and the scar that I had noticed the first time I met him stood out darkly on his cheek. We rattled across the iron bridge over the Voronezh river. For the last time I saw the whole city beneath me: the factory chimneys white against the sky, the fishermen in boats on the reservoir, the dome of the cathedral among the dilapidated wooden houses, and the mustard-coloured Stalinist blocks in the centre. It looked half-abandoned. Even the railway station was quiet.

That evening Emily and I stuffed the last few things into our cases and piled them onto the porters' cart in the yard. In the fading light the hostel, framed by shivering poplars, was almost attractive. We trailed past the rubbish dump, down Peace Prospect and through the line of babushkas still waiting by their buckets of boiled potatoes. Everyone was laughing and joking, as though this was just another train journey.

'When you come back, let's all go down to the Black Sea together,' Viktor suggested. 'Autumn's the time to go, September or October. It's beautiful –'

'Definitely,' we agreed. '*Otdykh!*'

'We'll meet you here on the platform and go straight on to the sea.'

'Yes! We'll celebrate right here, like this –'

'Let's drink to that.'

The shouts of Viktor and the girls were silenced as the train pulled away. We watched their mouths moving as they ran alongside us, waving and grinning. Only Mitya stood still, hands thrust deep into his pockets. Then he turned and walked away, hunching his shoulders.

Glossary

anglichanka (pl. **anglichanki**) – English girl
apparatchik – Soviet bureaucrat
babushka, babulya – grandmother, old woman
banya – steam bath
bomzh – acronym meaning homeless person
Bozhe moi! – My God!
budka – shed
dachnik (pl. **dachniki**) – owner of a dacha, a country house
dalshe – further
demi-sek – demi-sec, medium dry
dochka – daughter
dyevushka – girl
dyevka – girl (slightly derogatory)
dvushka – two-kopeck piece
elektrichka (pl. **elektrichki**) – small electric train for short
    journeys
entrakt – interval, from the French *entracte*
fortochka – the small casement that can be opened when the
    rest of the window is sealed up for winter

garderob – cloakroom, from the French *garderobe*

Gastronom – food store

golubka (pl. **golubki**) – female dove; a term of endearment

gorko! – bitter! A word shouted at weddings to make the bride and groom kiss, on the assumption that they should exorcise anything that is bitter or difficult on the first day of their marriage, and then everything will be sweet thereafter.

inostranets, inostranka – foreign man, woman

intelligent (pl. **intelligenty**) – intellectual, educated person. Pronounced with a hard 'g'.

Komendant – head of the hostel

kulich – traditional Easter cake

ladno – all right, OK

magizdat – underground copying and distribution of music that sprung up under Brezhnev, the equivalent of samizdat for books

mily, milaya, milenky – dear, darling

mutny – cloudy, opaque

nichevo – nothing, it's nothing

na brudershaft – from the German *Bruderschaft*. To drink a toast as brothers, with linked arms.

nu-ka, posmotrim – now, let's see

otdykh – rest, relaxation, holiday

papirosa (pl. **papirosy**) – Russian cigarettes of black tobacco with a long tube of cardboard for a filter

Pobeda – Victory (a Soviet make of car)

privyet – hello

propiska – residence permit

pukh – fluffy seed from a certain type of poplar

salo – salted pig fat

sek – sec, dry

shashlyk – kebabs

Slava Bogu! – Thank God!

smetana – sour cream

sovok – someone who lives according to the old Soviet ways (derogatory)

s prazdnikom! – Congratulations on whichever holiday it might be – Border Guard Day, International Labour Day, or First Day back at school.

ublyudki – bastards

Univermag – short for Universalny Magazin – department store

vakhtersha – concierge, janitor

vodochka – the affectionate diminutive for vodka

vytrezvitel – lock-up for drunks

yolki palki! – a jokey expression meaning whoops!

zakuski – snacks to eat with vodka

zefir – nutty meringues

Answers to exercises on pp. 78–9:
b) i)   the knitwear department
    ii) the shoe department
    iii) the ladies' underwear department
c) baraban – drum
    kolokol – bell
    skreepka – violin